TILES
for a beautiful home

TILES

Published 1989 by Merehurst Press
Ferry House, 51-57 Lacy Road, Putney,
London, SW15 1PR

© Copyright Tessa Paul 1989

© Copyright Merehurst Limited 1989
By arrangement with Dunestyle Publishing Ltd.

Co-published in Australia and New Zealand by
Child & Associates, Unit C, 5 Skyline Place,
Frenchs Forest, 2086, Australia.

Editor	Robyn Karney
Editorial Director	Megra Mitchell
Art Director	John Strange
Design	Strange Design Associates
Illustrations	K. Seppings
Typesetting	O'Reilly Clark, London
Origination	Reprocraft Ltd, London
	J. Film Process, Singapore

Printed in Italy by New Interlitho s.p.a., Milan

ISBN 1-85391-028-7

Cover Modern tile in the style of
William Morris. *The Tile Collection.*

Half title page Ornate Victorian tiled
porch panel.

Title page A selection of Victorian
tiles, including examples by William
De Morgan, Max Lauger,
W. B. Simpson, C. F. A. Voysey,
Walter Crane, John Hassall and
Lewis F. Day. *Phillips Fine Art
Auctioneers.*

Contents page Nine William De
Morgan tiles. *Phillips Fine Art
Auctioneers.*

TILES
for a beautiful home

Tessa Paul

Tessa Paul

MEREHURST PRESS
LONDON

CONTENTS

CHAPTER 1

Above and right The ancient Greeks developed an artistic ideal which has served as a model for centuries of Western art. Their design concepts were based on natural forms, abstracted to create a purely ornamental effect. These designs are still in use. In the bathroom scheme above, the classic *anthemion* or honeysuckle shape forms a visual focus between window and mirror. The tiles opposite carry a variation of the Greek *echinus* pattern. *Sally Anderson Tiles*.

Tiles are used to cover the surface of the United States space shuttle. No other material offers such sturdy protection to the space craft as it makes its wild and lonely journey through the galaxy, nor does any other fabric withstand the ferocious heat that overwhelms the shuttle as it re-enters the earth's atmosphere.

Nobody need quibble over the function and efficiency of tiling. Because tiles are water-resistant, heat-reflective and tough, they are, and have long been, widely used by architects in all kinds of building, from simple washrooms to imposing temples, and to cover roofs, floors and walls in shops, restaurants, offices and airports as well as in our own homes. And because tiles are made of ceramic, they are not only the builder's concern, but are included in the potter's craft, playing a part in the technical development of ceramics.

This covering, then, has a symbiotic relationship with architecture, and with pottery; yet the tile, an uneasy hybrid, moves nervously between these two disciplines. Art historians give tiles only a brief paragraph or two in the grand epic of architecture, and they abandon the prosaic shape of the tile to explore the fascinating variety offered by ceramic pots, jars, vases and dishes. Pity the art historian! Because the essential function of tiles is beyond dispute, it would be superfluous to repeat their purpose when referring to them as an architectural accessory, and it would be fraudulent to document the technical advance in ceramics as a 'history of tiles'. But this hybrid, the architectural ceramic called the tile, is greatly appreciated for its decorative value, and it is in the story of ornament that the tile finds its significant relationship.

'Ornament is Crime'

John Ruskin wrote that 'all architecture proposes an effect on the human mind, not merely a service to

Above Painters have turned their skills to ceramic tiles and have sought to move beyond simple decorative effects. This decorative tile panel has been inspired by Persian miniature paintings. *Carmona Tiles.*

the human frame'. The concept that architecture is purely functional is one that debases the human spirit. From necessity, man turned to building, but his need to embellish, to enrich with images and emblems, was as urgent as his need to make shelters. This emotional demand to adorn has an insistent, persuasive voice, although a strident, rebel tone has been heard in our own century. 'Ornament is crime,' announced Adolf Loos, the early twentieth century writer-architect, who embraced the concept of Functionalism. His view was not unique, but was supported by others who also believed that no adornment was required if the material used was perfectly suited to the function of the building. But the disciples of Functionalism ignored the fact that some materials, while compatible with function, are not necessarily pleasing and, indeed, cry out for embellishment.

In the earliest city we know, Jericho, first settled in about 7500 BC, the inhabitants constructed their buildings from mud. This material has facile plasticity; it can be shaped and moulded to suit its purpose, but it is drab. The people of Jericho transformed the mud by polishing the surface until they achieved a reddish plaster. They were, in effect, decorating with an early forerunner of the tile.

Haphazardly, miraculously, the tile developed to fulfil a functional need, although its inherent qualities did not offer any aesthetic appeal. However, this ceramic material does allow for rich embellishment and, very soon, tiles came to be prized for their ornamental value. The purpose, or intent, of ornament is important, and all decorative art falls naturally into one or other of two great divisions, the symbolic or the aesthetic. Images and embellishments make crucial statements and we should understand their purpose if we are to use

Below The basic function of tiles has not prevented artists from using the medium for realistic 'painterly' effects. The tiled wall surroundings on this indoor swimming pool has been transformed into a mysterious Edwardian fantasy scene.
Sally Anderson Tiles.

Below This design is an unusual combination of realistic and conceptual forms. The butterfly and leaf shapes are recognizable, but arranged into a purely decorative shape. *Sally Anderson Tiles.*

Right These charming, but not entirely realistic, insect and bird images are typical of the light sketches from nature used in Delft tile ornament *Castelnau Tiles*

them to their best advantage in the decoration of our homes. Our choice of a decorative motif is richer if we recognize and understand the appropriate use of the symbolic and the aesthetic in ornament.

'In the Beginning'

Drawing and painting were among our very first skills, developing side-by-side with the making of stone tools and weapons. Before we acquired literacy and constructed cities and social structures, prehistoric artists squatted deep within natural caves and subterranean tunnels where they painted the likenesses of animals, the bison and the deer, the powerful beasts who were the prey man hunted so relentlessly. The rough surfaces of these hidden places were adorned for symbolic purposes in a rite of magical compulsion, for the artists were also the hunters. With these images, they sought to placate the animals, their victims. 'We need to kill you, but look we have re-created you, your shape and your beauty; now you are immortal and you will return to us.' This was the plea contained in each and every rock painting, and the images were believed to give a protective blessing to both the hunted and the hunter. These early images were expressions of dark fear and awe, but were executed with loving sensitivity. This symbolism may be irrelevant to us nowadays, but the need to paint and adorn is rooted in this primitive urge to give tangible form to our emotional longings.

As paintings grew, twin-like, with the technology of tools, so adornment was inseparably linked to man's slowly developing progress as builder-architect. In the neolithic settlement of Catalhoyuk, Turkey, built in the seventh millenium BC, a realization of the plasticity of mud extends beyond its use in construction, into one of ornamental moulding. There, among the primitive huts, are the

holy shrines of these early people and again, in obeisance to a compulsion for images, individual panels are decorated with plaster relief.

At a religious site, Ggantija, in Malta, built in the third millenium, there are examples of detail not crucial to the function of the structural stone. A rich yellow limestone was included for colour effects and the inner wall suraces were patterned and textured by the use of simple tools.

What urgent symbolism demanded different colours and different textures from the functional materials? The answer, sensed so long ago, can only be guessed at from our perspective, but we must acknowledge the importance of symbolism in early embellishment.

The Visual Leap

Prehistoric rock paintings were spread haphazardly over the walls of caves, sometimes covering, even obscuring each other. In fragments of wall recovered from early fourth millenium Egyptian sites, we can discern paintings of men, animals, birds and ships scattered at random across the surfaces. There is no order in the jumbled and incoherent placing of the images. They are put down on any useful bit of surface. The primary and urgent artistic purpose was to fix the magical, symbolic likenesses of humans and animals and, thus, to ensure both creatures an immortal protection. It was believed that the images would appease the gods.

Sometime after this period, a transformation occurs in the artistic mind. Images no longer crowd or jostle, but are fitted into contrived and individual areas; the correlation between line and space has been realized. This miracle in visual perception happened at a remote period and created, of course, innovations in every artistic expression, but the principle effect on the decorative arts was the development of repetitive patterns arranged within a controlled space. It is impossible to define when or how this new perception took root. There are examples in Mesopotamia and Egypt in the fourth millenium, at

Right Repetitive patterns were profoundly to affect the organization and composition of ancient art forms. They were widely used as borders enclosing representational paintings, and as decoration in their own right.

a time when the social system in both these areas was evolving from a loose nomadic hunting life into settled agrarian community life. When a people chose to establish themselves in one place as a settled group, they found that they were compelled to divide the land into plots, of which each family claimed one as their own. Thus, a system of mathematics, with an understanding of the division of space, developed as part of the new social system. It is in this way that engineers may have provoked artists into a comprehension of controlled space.

Another hypothesis, put forward by René Huyghe, General Editor of the *Larousse Encyclopedia of Prehistoric and Ancient Art*, is worth quoting. He thinks that an element which may have been part of this 'visual innovation' was a technical accident in pottery. Even the earliest shards of pottery are incised with humble decoration, marks scratched on the surface in sharp or wavy lines, and Huyghe points out that, 'when the craftsman decorates the edge of a bowl with a zig-zag, he involuntarily creates a new figure which is only visible if he looks at his receptacle afterwards, not in profile, but in full face from underneath. In the circular form, which he then sees, the zig-zag forms a star . . .' The subtle effects of line and perspective, the unexpected change in form, provoked artistic development. Huyghe also says, 'the use of cylinder seals was especially widespread in Mesopotamia. The eye of the artist grew used to seeing the same theme repeated indefinitely.'

Early civilizations made extensive use of repetitive designs. Buildings, weapons, tools, utensils and textiles were adorned with pattern, but, because of the symbolic significance of the design, repetition was not confined to small-scale ornament. We see the majestic repetition of enormous figures, worked on glazed brick, on the great ziggurats of Mesopotamia, on the palaces of Susa and Babylon and, in Egypt, on temple walls. Often these figures were of high priests, royal kings or strange mythological beasts, all of whom were closely linked to the religious faith of the people. Although extremely beautiful and worked in a type of ceramic, these impressive decorations are hardly a suitable theme for the tiles we plan in our own homes, so we shall concentrate on the more demure and diverse border ornamentation achieved by these early cultures.

The Nature of Egypt

Tiles are often designed for use as borders enclosing a monochrome tiled area, and many of us prefer this arrangement in our kitchens and bathrooms – rooms in which utensils and gadgets, bottles and jars, are placed where they can be seen

Left and below Forms of ornament developed in the early civilizations of Mesopotamia, such as Assyria, were rhythmical, repetitive designs based on geometric principles. Their beautiful simplicity remains effective even when used to decorate very modern fittings.
Sally Anderson Tiles.

Right Greek artists developed designs based on the growth and movement of natural vegetation. This tile design, using a rhythmical design broken by flower shapes, retains this concept of natural growth. *Elon Tiles*

Below Islamic design is based on careful geometric principles. Traditional craftsmen used a flowing line which hid the subtle grid, but this modern interpretation makes the geometry very obvious. *The Tile Collection.*

and easily reached. Because all these objects take up space, there is a risk of creating an over fussy effect by using patterned tiles on the wall behind them. They generally look better when backed by monochrome tiling, perhaps surrounded by a patterned border, or one of contrasting colour.

Borders were an integral and widely used system of ornament in Egyptian art. These gloriously creative people patterned each and every surface, and their designs are delightful, balanced and pure in concept. We have found no traces of a literate artistic civilization before that of Egypt. We presume that it grew without influence from other cultures, that the Egyptian conceptual approach was entirely original, free of forms or theories borrowed from previous eras. This art found its inspiration in nature; the artistic principles from which it developed depended utterly upon the forms found in plants and animals. These people used glazed, enamelled brick more frequently than tiles, but these were a similar form of ceramic and achieved the flat, bright appearance of tiles. Red, blue and yellow, defined with black and white, were the principal colours, with the occasional use of green and purple.

The Egyptians used conceptual realism in their work, which means that they depicted the basic form, the essential structure of a plant, representing the idea, rather than the reality, of the object, so that we are not presented with a lotus blossom carefully drawn and shaded to imitate reality, but are given the design of the blossom. We can see the essential shape of plants reproduced in the heavy stone architecture of Egypt. The groves of papyrus that flourished in the Nile Valley were cut down for use in the construction of pre-stone buildings, and when the builders progressed to stone structures, they simply copied the shape of the papyrus when

Below In this border a classic style has been created in the combination of geometric pattern and an abstract floral form. *Fired Earth.*

they made a stone column. The long triangular-shaped stalks were carved out of stone, although magnified hugely to suit new proportions, and the circle of foliage at the top of the stalk became the basis for the design of the capital on the stone column. These ancient artists comprehended the rhythmic and symmetrical laws of nature. They observed that in plants a central stem supports a series of branches and leaves which curve upwards and away from this stem. Even the structure of a leaf follows this rule and the Egyptians did not deviate from this rule in the design of their ornament. We

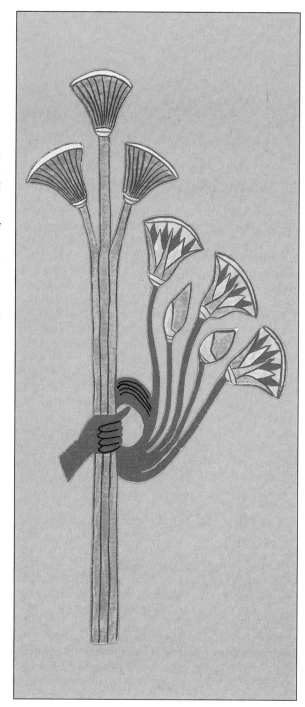

Right A variation of the papyrus reveals the subtle conceptual realism which guided the artists of ancient Egypt.

can observe this principle in the papyrus image which is drawn in a variety of shapes: short and thick or tall and thin, but never varying in the basic natural design.

It is this obeisance to the natural laws of growth that gives Egyptian design its satisfactory sense of balance. We are never disturbed or dismayed by their ornament because the conceptual principles are based on the symmetry of natural form.

Despite the fact that we are referring to an art that is almost 6,000 years old, it is not an altogether bizarre idea to have an 'Egyptian' theme in your home. This is not to encourage a bathroom designed to look like a movie set for a Cleopatra epic, but a serious invitation to look at the beautiful ornamentation of Egypt and to adapt it so that it is artistic, interesting, and entirely suitable to your bathroom. If you are fascinated by plant forms and their design potential, if you are intrigued by the symbolism granted by the Egyptians to certain plants, then this style of ornament is worth serious consideration. Individual tiles, representing a lotus blossom or the disc of the sun, organized within the otherwise monochrome surround to the bath with a border which uses the same motif, will give your bathroom a style which is both beautiful and evocative. Of course, the theme must be sustained throughout, with light covers, floor tiles and fittings all contributing to a discrete Egyptian style. Tiles selected to depict the tall papyrus stem and its gently curving leaves, following the Egyptian convention, would create an ornamental accessory in harmony with the shower area.

A study will soon dispel the superficial notion that strange 'side-ways' people, papyrus stalks, lotus blossom and pyramids make up the total of Egyptian art. Their use of geometric form in borders and ornaments is extremely varied and inventive.

Below In Egypt the artists referred to the real plant for their ornamental designs, and this modern designer has created a tile decoration which used the Egyptian motifs as a design source. *Sally Anderson Tiles.*

The zig-zag, the square, the diamond and the triangle are presented in a hundred different combinations, mixtures and blends. A careful survey of this geometric rhythm presents another possible cause for that 'visual leap' which perceived the relationship between space and line. The geometry often follows the rhythm created by the warp and weft of weaving, and basket weaving is a very ancient skill. The arrangement of the reeds can be varied and surprising, developing not so much from a conscious design in the craftsman's mind, but from necessity and improvization. To quote Owen Jones: 'The formation of pattern through [basket] weaving would give a rising people the first notions of symmetry, arrangement, and the disposition of masses.'

Many primitive art forms all over the world reveal an intricate understanding of geometric ornament, which can be directly related to the patterns created involuntarily in basket weaving. None that we know of achieved the high art of the Egyptians. Many tile patterns manufactured today use the numerous borders and patterns devised by the Egyptians, although the modern designer may be quite unaware of his debt to this ancient heritage.

Below and bottom Ornamental forms were devized by the earliest artists and craftsmen. Their primary design source was the shape of plants, blossoms, leaves and waves, followed by an understanding of geometric repetition. Contemporary designers may not be fully aware of their debt to these distant civilizations, but modern manufacturers use tile patterns which can be traced directly to ancient sources. The two pictures below represent geometric wave designs, reminiscent of Cretan ornamentation. *The Tile Collection.*

Right The curving line of this floral scroll may also have been inspired by the waves of the sea and has been used here to ornament a bathroom. *Fired Earth.*

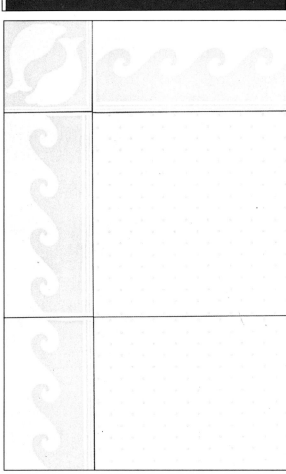

A Sea Change

The art in Egypt, beautiful, natural and balanced, was nevertheless fixed into a rigid system of rules, dominated by religious belief. Artists were not allowed to diverge from certain immutable laws. For instance, to indicate the movement of a person walking, a painter had always to depict the left foot forward, never the right, and kings were represented as much larger than other people. It was also an art dedicated to the worship of death, although not in a morbid sense. This was, after all, a culture preoccupied by the notion of an after-life.

Egyptian graphic work, then, was symbolic; it continued those primeval hopes and pleas first expressed by the prehistoric artist. This symbolic purpose can be seen in the arts of Mesopotamia, among the Babylonian, Sumerian and Assyrian peoples. Their work, too, was dominated by their religious beliefs. They were not as artistic as the Egyptians and borrowed much from the people of the Nile. Following their masters, they adhered to natural forms, but the rendering was neither as clear nor as balanced, perhaps because it was learnt rather than instinctively felt.

Their building methods were different, too, in that they relied on mud and brick where the Egyptians used stone. The Mesopotamian cultures made much wider use of glazed brick and kiln-fired tiles, and their colours were blue, red, green, orange, white and black. Not a great deal of their ornamentation has been found because of the nature of the material used, but their designs are similar to those of Egypt.

The Assyrians liked the effect of black outlines, which led them to employ a strong emphasis on line and, in one of their patterns we find, for the first time, a loose curve fitted into a geometric base, a very early forerunner of the beautiful and complex

arabesque tile designs of the Arabs.

The convention of employing religious symbolism controlled the early Mediterranean civilizations for centuries, but the first signal of artistic liberty from priestly domination is seen in the Aegean culture of the Minoans in Crete. This is not to imply that the Minoans were without faith or superstition, but, in their culture, there is a remarkable rarity of temples, or stone statues of 'higher' beings, which may indicate the lack of a strongly institutionalized religion.

The Minoan people were essentially seafarers; from their island base, their ships radiated out towards Asia Minor or Mesopotamia, to Egypt, to the Greek mainland, and even further afield. (An example of Cretan metalwork has even been found in Cornwall.) The sea is an unpredictable and irascible element; it forces those who travel upon it to expect unreliable, ever-changing conditions. A

seafarer does not think in orderly, geometric lines in the way a land-owning farmer might. His gods are temperamental and volatile, rather than fixed and solid beings. Crete owes much to the Egyptian artistic heritage. The Minoans retained many of the conventions, especially those of portraying people in the familiar Egyptian full-frontal pose with profile head and the use of different colours to discriminate between men and women. The Cretan observation of animals, also, was as sensitive and loving as the Egyptians', who were not strait-jacketed by priestly laws governing the way animals were depicted.

However, Cretan ornament was altogether looser and freer than the geometric designs of her impressive neighbour. The spiral was an obsessive theme with these island people: the spiral which they saw in the churning sea around them, in the whorled shells on their beaches, in the creatures of

Right A sample of floor tiles which show a basic pattern created from a simple geometric format, and offering a Greek *key* design as a border. *Paris Ceramics.*

the deep, the octopus and the squid. It became the basis of their ornamentation, and inward spirals, reversed spirals and undulations replaced the harsher zig-zag of Egypt and Mesopotamia. The joyous, convoluted spiral of Crete was to be absorbed and re-created by seafaring peoples in Scandinavia, in England, in Ireland and in the Baltic countries. Slowly, in imitation of the island Minoans, the intricate Viking and Celtic patterns developed to reach their zenith a thousand years later. But the complicated knots and whorls based on the spiral are essentially suited to the malleability of metal, to the enhancement of jewellery, belt buckles, sword trimmings and daggers; they do not sit easily on ceramic, being too intricate to be reproduced properly in this material. Perhaps this is why the tiles found on Minoan sites were not decorated in loose ornamental fashion, but used a more severe graphic style to depict the Cretan landscape.

The free-flowing line persuaded the Cretans to give more movement to their wall-paintings and frescoes. Undeterred by priests, and expressing a joyful love of life and nature, they created an art that was, as Claude Schaeffer says, 'a spectacle for the eyes, a visual pleasure'. More significantly, he adds, 'Let us take careful note: a primitive era of art is over: it assumes a meaning, hitherto unknown, which it is not to lose again'. Art was no longer confined to a religious or superstitious expression. This step, out of the symbolic world and into the aesthetic, was to lead towards the brilliant era of an art dictated by humanism and a pure delight in the beauty of the world: that of the Greeks.

Gifts from the Greeks

Hellenic architecture is not conspicuous for its use of tiles, although the Greeks knew how to make sun-

Below left A Greek *key* design used
as a border decoration.
The Tile Collection.

Below The *key*, used so widely in
ancient Greece, is still a favourite
border ornament, and Greek line-
drawings have been copied on the
tiled walling further to emphasize the
design theme of this room.
Sally Anderson Tiles.

dried building bricks. Marble was preferred as a
building material, especially in public architecture,
and decoration was carved from, and painted onto,
the marble. This is not the place to elaborate on the
majesty and perfection of Greek architecture and
sculpture to be found in the achievements of the
Hellenic world: the Akropolis, the Discus Thrower,
the statue of Poseidon, the temple at Delphi, among
others. When we think of these timeless creations,
we tend to forget the detail of Greek art and we
neglect the rich contribution the Greeks made to the
decorative arts through their ceramics and
ornament. Owen Jones observed that, 'from the

very abundant remains we have of Greek ornament,
we must believe the presence of refined taste was
almost universal and that the land was overflowing
with artists whose hands and minds were so trained
as to enable them to execute these beautiful
ornaments with unerring truth.'

The Hellenics did not abandon nature as a design
source, but their approach differed from that of the
Egyptians. The latter civilization reduced the plant
to the components of its basic shape; they
understood the *design* of nature. The Greeks
realized the *principles* of nature and their rendering
of a plant was imbued with a sense of vitality. Greek

Below The drawing on this Greek vase is not easily adapted to modern use, but the border patterns which surround it are of great interest.

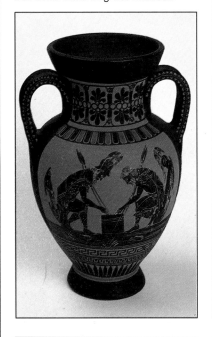

Above This tile border uses the *anthemion* interspersed with an abstract design of a corolla. Both forms are designs used in ancient Greece. *The Tile Collection.*

Right The illustration shows the basic Greek *echinus* and *guilloche* designs.

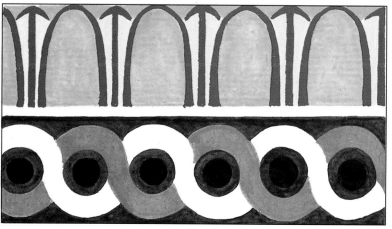

foliage may resemble the laurel or the ivy, but the line is decorative rather than imitative. Patterns and border designs on Greek ceramics surround the principle images on jars, vases and dishes. The main designs are usually scenes from myths and legends, episodes in the lives of heroes, adventures of the numerous gods and goddesses, athletes and hunters. All these are depicted in flawless line-work of a grace and beauty rarely achieved with pen and ink, let alone in the complicated process of pottery. As F. Edward Hulme sums it up: 'The best designs are depicted in monochrome, being simple in character and of great dignity in treatment'.

If the principle design of a Greek jar is so lovely, why would one wish to seek the incidental embellishments? The obvious answer is that the gods, heroes and myths, no matter how beautifully contrived on the jars and plates, are neither suitable nor relevant to a modern choice of tile design. This is the dilemma presented by Greek ceramic ware. The very beauty of the work, inspired by an artistic grace and skill, holds a universal appeal, but the subjects are rooted in symbolism and an obscure cultural grammar. They confront us with a problem which requires an understanding of the division in decorative art between the symbolic and the purely aesthetic. The Greeks made consistent use of ornamental forms, and anyone purchasing tiles today will find these forms reproduced in modern tile design. It helps the discerning customer to make an informed choice if, when confronted by the wide range offered by modern tile production, he or she has a knowledge of Greek ornament and its visual intent. The most ordinary and ancient forms of ornament, such as the zig-zag and the *guilloche*, are used extensively in Hellenic decoration. These forms are universal and are found in the work of the

earliest Egyptians, African tribes and the people of Oceana. Their enduring popularity is due to the utter simplicity of their line, a line that offers, in the zig-zag, different visual effects if placed vertically, horizontally or diagonally. The *guilloche* allows a changing emphasis in weight and mass, a wide variation in light and shade. The Greeks understood all these nuances and used them to full effect. They made the *key* peculiarly their own and revealed great ingenuity in varying the right-angled line to create many forms of keywork. Hellenic ornament made wide use of the *anthemion* or honeysuckle design and we tend to think of this form, too, as a typically Greek decoration. It is a beautiful

Below Light brush strokes and fresh colour create a graceful floral ornament. *Castelnau Tiles.*

decoration with an irresistible vitality in its radiating and upsweeping lines. Another much favoured design was the *echinus*, with its contrast of curved shapes and sharp lines.

These are the ornamental forms most widely used in Hellenic ceramics, architectural moulding, fresco borders and floors. They are aesthetic forms which rely on a repetitive sequence to give consequence to the design and this makes them as relevant today as they were through centuries of decorative art.

A Sense of Ornament

Think carefully about symbolism before you select your tile design. That athlete, with a hare racing at his heels, reproduced in the characteristic red and black of Greek ceramic, may make you stop and wonder at its perfection, but it is unlikely to harmonize with your kitchen wall. The strange and fascinating figure with a jackal head, painted so delightfully on the Egyptian sarcophagus, will, I assure you, look very odd on the patio floor! These are both ornaments of great symbolic value, representing a hero and god respectively. With Egyptian decoration, the symbolism is extremely formal and powerful, but to the modern eye and mind, this hybrid jackal-man is a bizarre concept. Placed in your own home, it is liable to provoke a nervous giggle from the unwary visitor. The Greek image is much more subtle. It is neither bizarre nor formal in its symbolism. It shows a recognizable man with a familiar animal. We love it for its beauty, but this fellow and his hare would stand uneasily trapped in a tile in an apartment block kitchen. He is too rich in association with the ancient Hellenic world, he is too proud and archaic and symbolic of an airy world of playful gods and heroic supermen. In short, it would be pretentious to introduce such an important cultural note in a modern room.

This means that the ornament of a building, and especially of your home, cannot be easily borrowed or stolen from other cultural sources, unless the visual intent of the decoration is fully understood. Of course, the symbols of other cultures *can* be used, but they must be modified to express a modern statement, otherwise they will impress only as awkward or even mawkish. Make your symbolism your own. If you use the gods of another culture, you cannot express yourself because such ornament will be perceived as an essentially religious statement of that culture and not as something relevant to you. It is wiser to ransack patterns taken from designs of the inanimate or of an abstract style, which you can arrange to create a new symbolism of significance to you and your family, and to the room you are tiling. Plant, animal and bird motifs are always popular and are traditionally powerful and emotional symbols. Beware, however, of decorating with the image of the sphinx or the gryphon!

The Egyptian abstract of a papyrus, the lotus design or the globe, all held a deep symbolic value in that culture. Today, they remain simple, beautiful and not at all bizarre. They are natural shapes, familiar to all of us, and therefore suitable to our lives. The lotus represented life and growth, the papyrus indicated the intellect, and the globe was, of course, the mighty sun. These were the values the Egyptians gave them; we may have a different feeling for these forms. For you, the lotus blossom may mean luxury and pleasure and, for that

Below The size of this tiled wall surround to a swimming pool is not suited to a repetitive decoration. Instead, the designer has transformed the wall into a romantic tile landscape which gives the pool a dreamy, classic dimension. *Sally Anderson Tiles.*

Right These wall 'paintings' are not detailed or painterly in their rendering, but use a bold, graphic line to make an original decoration in an extensively tiled breakfast room. *Sally Anderson Tiles.*

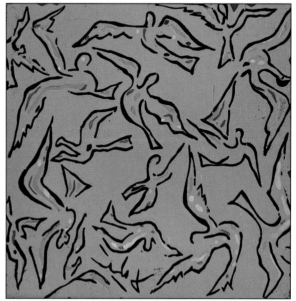

Below Artists have been inspired to encroach on the potter's art. These are designs from the Surrealist painter, Salvador Dali. *Fired Earth*.

meaning, you choose to have these blossoms decorate your bathroom. Or they may conjure up water and river banks in your imagination and you place them, appropriately, on the tile surround to a swimming pool.

With a discreet and stylish use of this Egyptian motif, but not of the strange gods and beasts unique to that land, you can create an ornamentation that acknowledges its cultural source, yet is able to exist as an aesthetic statement, even as it holds a private symbolism for you. There are so many designs which offer you the opportunity of giving your decoration both a symbolic and aesthetic value. You must be aware of what you want to say with your ornamentation. Perhaps you want to include a particular fruit motif in your kitchen tiling, because it symbolizes something for you; or perhaps you view your kitchen as an efficient work place and a clean, sharp zig-zag design will express this functional outlook. The kitchen may also be a

Right The intricate lines of Islamic art weave a complex arabesque of dense patterns which can be seen covering the tiled walls of mosques throughout the Arab world.
Leighton House.

Below Tiny ceramic cubes create a design of charming simplicity.

family room and the ornament is chosen to reveal that family life. The enormous choice of fruit designs, geometric borders and animal motifs in the tiles available today, allows you to find the exact symbolism to express yourself through your home.

While concentrating on the visual intent of your ornamental tiles the practical and functional aspects must also be considered. Is the design suited to the material? Does the decoration fit intrinsically with the shape and texture of the tile? Perhaps, like the convoluted knot designs of the Celts and Vikings, the design is ill-adapted to tiling. Celtic knots are so intricate and closely woven that they not only look awkward and technically inconsiderate but the flowing, complex line is disrupted by the edge-to-edge patterning that controls the grouping of tiles. If you require ornate decoration, there are complicated designs which embrace or absorb the edged lines of the tiles, the most famous and lovely being the arabesque loops of the Arabs.

Look and consider carefully how tiling is laid and constructed and how well, or badly, the design suits tiling, before making a decision on the motif you prefer.

After the Greeks

After the glory of the Hellenic period, the northern Mediterranean cultures assume decorative forms not altogether sympathetic to the ornament of tiling. The Romans were not an artistic race; their skills lay in engineering, warfare and administration, and in their architecture and other art forms they borrowed heavily from the Greek culture which they ultimately overwhelmed. But Roman ornament lacked the refinement of Greek, and their designs tended to be over-worked and superfluous, even ill-adapted to the purposes for which they were used. The Greek and Egyptian

principle of connecting lines flowing from a central stem, was abused by the Romans. They allowed scrolls to grow out of scrolls, which flowed and circled round plant forms and so achieved an effect of ornate fussiness.

In Pompeii, we have a superb site for the study of Roman design, and, in Pompeii, there is a lack of discipline, revealed in the looseness of the painter's hand which has lost the guidance of a sound artistic form. There are many charming frescoes done in this capricious manner, but they would not fit the parameters set by the requirements of tiling.

Out of old pagan Rome, a great Christian empire bloomed, based in Byzantium, which is now Istanbul in modern Turkey. The Byzantines absorbed artistic influences from Rome and the East, but developed a formalism entirely their own. In their decoration they preferred a thin interlaced patterning as against geometric form and when geometric forms do appear in Byzantine art, their

close, tight detail makes them more suited to the paint work of frescoes, or to the chips of mosaic work. The predominant feature of Byzantine art is that it is a symbolic art. Every building, candlestick, ornament was dedicated to, and created for, the Christian faith. In Byzantium, Justinian I built an enormous church, Santa Sophia. It still exists and is now used as an Islamic mosque, but it was created by a Christian Byzantine emperor and it is a beautifully ornamented, magnificently designed building erected to the glory of God.

All over the Empire, churches were built; in Syria, in the Baltic, in Italy. All held interiors of dazzling glass mosaics, richly coloured and patterned and used to portray the lives of the saints, the Apostles, the Virgin and Jesus. Byzantine art was held firmly within its religious vision and these splendid mosaics use gold, blue and red to emphasize this vision. The mosaics were used on the walls and covered great soaring domes which glittered and shifted in the muted church light. The Romans also excelled in mosaic work, but they preferred to apply it to pavements and flooring. Tiling and mosaic are put to similar uses in wall and floor coverings, but the design of a mosaic does not transfer easily to tiling. The visual intent of a mosaic is quite different from that of tiling. Mosaics are made from thousands of little bits of stone, glass or ceramic. All these pieces, with their tiny surfaces, cause an unevenness of texture, enhanced by light refraction. The mosaic artist anticipates these effects and uses them to describe his design.

The tile is, in comparison, a large, flat surface. It does not connect freely to its fellows, but tile is laid against tile in geometric precision, straight edge meeting straight edge in an angular convention. This is the diaper of tiling and, combined with the technical considerations of ceramic, it renders the

CHILDRENS
TOY BOOKS

Left A tile panel carries an image composed of clear, graphic lines. The bold composition is well-suited to the purpose of advertisement.
W. H. Smith.

tile incapable of producing the same effect as a mosaic. This may seem like an obvious statement, but it is not unknown for some designers to move a decoration suited to one medium and plonk it carelessly onto another.

To All Intents

The Romans, in their mosaic work, used a style of realistic representation to portray battle scenes, the life of the gods, their emperors, or simply scenes of everyday life. There are pictures of farmers, fishermen and housewives, interspersed with bowls of food, fruit, animals, birds and fishes. They laid many mosaic pavements, but one of their most famous wall mosaics shows Alexander the Great in battle against Darius III, King of Persia.

The Byzantine style is quite different. Their art was formalised and people were portrayed in an elongated and elegant style.

We can find modern mosaic work in Mexico City, Israel and elsewhere. We may see vast designs across the facades of buildings, depicting a landscape or a city-scape, mosaics in lobby interiors symbolizing a company or its founder and pavement mosaics commemorating a public event. These are subjects the mosaic can carry. In mosaic the line is created by colour, which is controlled by, and set against, another colour. The line can curve and twist and move freely; its expression is scarcely inhibited. The light glitters and bounces off the numerous surfaces. A portrait done in mosaic is lent its liveliness and vitality by the behaviour of light. A landscape moves with the light and shadow playing on the mosaic and, added to this, there is a certain roughness of texture that suits the scene.

There *are* modern mosaic tiles available that are compatible with domestic use. Those which, for

example, employ predominant sea-greens and blues – sometimes linking together to form an image such as a fish – can add a touch of imaginative and attractive texture and colour to bathrooms, outdoor patios or portico walls.

Tiling cannot achieve the same effect as mosaic. There are various problems with pictorial representation in tiles, that are worth pointing out. For example, a landscape, carried across several tiles, has its line regularly dissected by the edges of tiles. The line stops at the edge of one tile and then resumes on the edge of the next tile. This may result in a clumsy horizon. The human form can present its problems as well. Limbs may be broken up between

Top These tiles have been illustrated with a bright still life that would be appropriate if used as a decoration in the kitchen or breakfast room. *Sylvia Robinson.*

Left A kitchen dominated by white needs the relief of some colour. The gentle pastels of this fruit basket make a pleasing visual focus. *Lambeth Tiles.*

Below The Victorians and Edwardians used tile panels extensively to mark pubs, shops and public buildings. Hard-wearing and easy to maintain, the tile is perfect for such use. Here a tile panel directs shoppers to a particular department. *W. H. Smith.*

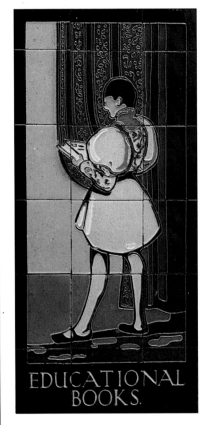

Right A different approach to tile decoration is depicted in the exaggerated floral ornament which gives a luxurious surround to this bathroom. *Sally Anderson Tiles.*

Left A modern tile 'painting' opens a closed tile wall with a garden scene viewed through a window. This quaint method of tile decoration allows a wide choice in interior design decisions. *Sylvia Robinson*.

Below This bookstore used tiles to great effect. Here is another delightful scene announcing a special department within the shop. *W. H. Smith*

several tiles and the trunk may be distorted by the horizontal and vertical lines. Tiles are less suited to painterly effects and more suited to strong, bold line representation, since the tile is hardly comparable to a huge, blank canvas. However, there are some remarkable examples of the human form stretched across a large area of tiles. Some of these are to be found in the Hall of Charles V in Seville, Spain. There are also Italian examples, where the Virgin Mary and her visitor, the Archangel, are divided up with an elbow in one square, a hand in another. Even heads do not escape the dividing line, so that eyes glower over an edge above the nose and an ear hangs a line away from the face.

The Victorians, too, delighted in working on tile the kind of realistic scene ususally associated with paint upon canvas, or even with mosaic work. These earnest, busy craftsmen spread pictures across vast areas of tile in order to produce the effect of a painting or fresco. Today there is still a busy industry, concentrated mainly in Holland, that creates panels of tiles painted intricately with scenes of quaint homesteads, thrilling seascapes and picturesque street scenes. One place where an illustration carried over a large tiled area looked particularly striking, was the children's ward at St Thomas's Hospital, in London. The Royal Doulton tiled walls were tough and easily maintained to high standards of hygiene. Large panels depicted scenes from fairy tales. Here, decoration was compatible with function.

But, to continue our discussion of ornament, let us turn to Islam and the Arabs.

Arabesques and Ottomans

The Islamic faith developed in the sixth century under the inspired teachings of the Prophet Mohammed. His first followers were in Arabia, but

BOOKS FOR COLLECTORS

the faith quickly spread across the Middle East, Asia Minor and North Africa and was, quite often, taken to these areas through military conquest.

The Arabs, a fierce nomadic race, had little artistic tradition of their own and absorbed the methods of other cultures. The Byzantines, for

Right Islamic ornament is mainly decorative, and not often realistic or symbolic. Significance is brought to the design through the use of Arabic script, which was included in the ornament and is usually a text from the Holy Koran. *Leighton House.*

instance, gave the new religion an artistic and cultural heritage which affected it for generations, and the Persians, quickly converting to the faith, brought their own extremely artistic culture to the service of Islam. Both these traditions gave an emphasis to the ornamental and both relied upon a symbolic rendering of their world. These elements were retained in the developing Islamic artistic form and were to flower into a unique Islamic style.

There is a curious conformity in Islamic art which allows its style to be recognized and repeated by peoples as diverse as the Moors in Spain or the Persians. Such unity cannot be attributed to a shared faith. Christians shared a common faith, but different countries still managed to produce styles distinctive to each nation. However, Christians spoke in many tongues and had different alphabets. All Muslims shared the Arab script, the ornamental and beautiful calligraphy of Islam, and all could identify with the ideas expressed in that script. Another theory behind this conformity is that the Koran, the holy book of Islamic teaching, expressly forbids the likeness of the human form to be re-created by artists. Any people, faced by such a restriction as this on their artistic expression, would be compelled to seek comfort in devising an endless variety of ornament. But authorities on the Koran differ in their information and, certainly, Muslim Moghuls in India did not pay much heed to the rule.

Whatever motivated Islamic art to follow a particular direction, this culture certainly excelled in ornamentation. Their designs are based on a diagonal interlacing and are rendered with precision, but not stiffness. Owen Jones, in his 'Grammar of Ornament', presents mathematical diagrams which reveal the thoughtful and regular symmetry of the intricate curves of Islamic work, based on geometric principles. The narrative line

Below The Islamic faith does not allow images of the human form, and the artist developed a highly creative approach to pattern, yet always used a geometric grid as a foundation to the design. *Leighton House.*

Below Islamic ornamental tiles cover roofs and walls with dense design. This rich artistic style may not suit modern design demands, but beautiful details such as this panel can be used in contemporary interiors. *Leighton House.*

can always be traced back with unbroken continuity to the root line; the scroll was transformed into a continuous line that contained and expressed foliate forms. (Unlike, for example, the Greeks, who placed their foliage so that it 'grew' from the line).

Islam had a fondness for complex design and a dread of empty spaces. Their curving lines. built with geometric precision, cross in an intricate weave of delicate loops and arabesques. The vacuum contained within each curve was filled by abstract or foliate forms. These designs are beautiful when reproduced in a tile panel, or as a border, and some make splendid floor designs. Some Muslim artists carried this dread of the vacuum into an obsession. Great mosques rear up in the barren lands of Samarkand covered, from soaring dome to solid ground level, in a glittering and ornate sheath of ornamental tiling. The Gur Emir, the mausoleum for the Emperor Tamerlaine, looms up in brilliant blue and green tiles, shining in barbaric splendour under a powerful sun. Persia is littered with examples of densely patterned tiling covering entire buildings, inside and out. The eye and the mind retreat from this rich, obsessive ornament. The subtle weaving lines turning continually within and without each other in a vast, endless maze, stupefy the eye and disturb the intellect. The longing for repose and peaceful space is overwhelming, and both are found later in Islamic history, in Moorish Spain and Ottoman Turkey.

So much has been written about the glorious achievements of the Islamic Moors in Spain that, to say anything of the Alhambra or the mosque in Cordova seems superfluous. It is enough to remark that, in Spain, the mysterious and complex ideals of Islam found their perfect expression. And besides, for adaptation to modern tiles, Ottoman Turkey yields a treasure house of relevant ornament. The

artists here turned, in time-honoured fashion, to nature as a design source and created decorations of a serene and delicate beauty. The predominant theme is one of flowers: tulips, roses, hyacinths and carnations decorate their tiles. Although each flower clearly suggests its species, it is rendered with formal understanding. Like the ancient Egyptians, Ottoman ceramicists translated the design of the plant and turned it into poetic ornament. Stems form a curving tracery, interspersed with feathery petals or a beautifully formed calyx. A border of dense, formal foliage encloses a pattern of abstract delicacy and all are worked in joyous blues, reds and greens. Many examples of Ottoman floral tile design can be translated into ornament for a modern home. They make a charming, decorative feature of the tiles in a small guests' lavatory, or can be fitted as a superb panel within the monochrome background used in a bathroom.

Victorian manufacturers carefully reproduced entirely 'natural' looking flowers on their tiles, in a design scheme which had moved away from the understanding of ornamentation perfected by the Ottomans. However, the Art Nouveau craftsmen, who followed the Victorians, conceived the purpose of ornament quite differently and reverted to a use of stylized, non-naturalistic design that had more in common with the Ottomans.

Today, we find a trend for the naturalistic and realistic representation growing again among manufacturers. Detailed representations of blossom and roses constitute many of the tile designs available today.

CHAPTER 2

Above The tightly controlled designs of Islam are worked out according to geometric principles. This modern adaptation reveals a looser line and a freer use of colour than any traditional ceramicist would have employed. *Carmona Tiles*.

Opposite Animals are not easily reduced to ornamental forms, but imaginary beasts or quaint depictions can be used to some effect. Here, a medieval version of the lion has been copied to create an unusual tile design. *Paris Ceramics*.

There is a curious kinship between artists that transcends political and social systems. The Muslims advanced in ceramic technology because, in the eighth century, the Persians captured some Chinese soldiers after a battle on the Eastern banks of the River Onyx. These prisoners-of-war introduced white Ting porcelain to their captors and taught them some of the techniques practised by Chinese potters. Thus Persians developed a passion for ceramics which influenced all the Islamic world. The Persians moved from tin-glazing and slip-painting into techniques of under-glaze painting. They learnt how to make lustre ware and extended their colour palette to blues, greens, purples, yellows and blacks. Islamic craftsmen excelled in their tile experiments, producing squares, rectangles, crosses, star shapes and tiles with relief designs, tiles with cut out lace patterns and tiles of rich decoration.

For centuries, waves of crusaders trekked across Europe to do holy battle against Islam and were fascinated by the architecture and ornament of the enemy. When they returned from the Holy Land, they did not forget what they had seen and learnt. In thirteenth century England, for instance, there was quite a vogue for tiling, inspired by the crusaders' descriptions and enthusiasm. This vogue lasted through the three hundred years of crusading. The returning soldiers did not bring back full information on the ceramic technology and English medieval tiles have a limited palette of brown, yellow, olive green and black. The swirling arabesques of Islam were modified by the Europeans and a distinctive Norman ornament developed, which was a nice mixture of Celtic scrolls and twisting loops combined with sharp geometrics – the zig-zag, or chevron as the Normans named it – and diamond shapes.

CERAMIC PICTURES

Right The designer must be wary of trying to modify the lively character of animals into a repetitive pattern. This gentle approach with soft colour and blurred outline, showing one creature on each tile, is a perfect design solution.

English tiles, in their limited but subtle palette, were of a fine, subdued beauty. Many very good examples still exist in the British Museum and *in situ* in cathedrals and abbeys. The Normans explored with great thoroughness the design potential of floor coverings and their craftsmen are memorable for their original portrayal of animals and birds. They learnt from the Celts, who delighted in zoomorphic ornament and, like the Celts, they would slip these creatures into their wood and stone carvings, their embroideries and manuscripts – and their tiles. The animals were rendered in a naive, sometimes grotesque, style, but their charm is timeless and they can be used in the ornament of our homes today.

The Normans did not confine their work to England, of course, and they were a major force in the development of the Romanesque style throughout Europe; similar tile coverings and little animal motifs can be found in France, Italy and Sicily.

Birds and Beasts

Animals have been painted and sculpted since man understood the connections between eye, mind and hand. Animals and birds have been given symbolic roles, or presented in their relationship to man as his victim, his friend, his adversary and his god. Every culture has produced images of the animals in its environment and, in most cases, it has been because the artists have had much pleasure and interest in observing the movement and habits of the mysterious animal lives around them. Yet rarely has the animal been reduced to a symmetrical, repetitive form in the decorative arts. There is something abhorrent in reducing living creatures to a formula, the kind of design that fits a lotus blossom, and few artists have tried to do so.

For most of us, our direct connection with animals is confined to our pet dog or cat, yet we are charmed by animal images and like to see them around us. A series of cat tiles, in a kitchen or on a patio wall, can make an interesting conversation piece. Elephants, foxes, episodes from Aesop's Fables – any animal, or animal group – rendered on a tile which is then placed as if at random within the tile area, gives a lively animated touch to the decor. And, of course, animals still carry a symbolism: as cunning as a fox, as strong as a horse, man's best friend, and so on . . .

The Egyptians, expressing themselves in one area which their priests did not regulate, have left superb images of closely observed animal life, while the Cretans, Romans and Greeks painted birds and animals with acute sensitivity. Some Islamic artists interpreted the Koran as placing a taboo on animal as well as human images, but the Persians and the Moghul artists felt no such inhibitions. For instance, they have left paintings of numerous hunting scenes, involving elephants, horses, camels, dogs and deer, all rendered with sprightly grace. Our choice of animal images, as we ransack the cultures of the world, is endless, but perhaps the Japanese offer the

Below This tile decoration follows principles established by Dutch ceramicists in the seventeenth century. A free hand brush drawing is painted in each tile, using a limited palette. These are then placed in a spacious arrangement confined by a border. *Fired Earth.*

CERAMIC PICTURES

Below Japanese designers have created superb graphic images of birds and animals. Western artists in the last century were heavily infuenced by Japanese work. This tile design shows the bold, linear and 'flat' effect which Europe learnt from Japan. *Royal Doulton Ltd.*

most perfect interpretations.

Japanese animal studies are potent in their simplicity of treatment, boldness of draughtsmanship and loving observation of their subject. The innate sense of composition and of balanced design makes the work of the Japanese artists eminently suited to tile decoration. But you may prefer the less conscious charm of more primitive artists: the Celtic craftsmen, whose quaint, clumsy studies sometimes make the animal difficult to identify, an Eskimo carving of a walrus, or the simple curve of a hippo, drawn by an African hand.

All these are suited to the purpose of ornament, for they are rendered with conceptual realism, whereas the natural realism of Egypt, Greece or Rome may present too painterly a quality for the visual intent of tiling. There are tile manufacturers and craft potters producing lovely renderings of animals. Such tiles are to be used as individual statements, as images that you enjoy on your walls, and not in repetitive rows. Although animals generally do not make good decorative patterns for the designer, birds can be organized into ornamental forms. Perhaps it is the shape of flight, the graceful uplifted wings that are ornamental in themselves, or perhaps we are accustomed to seeing them in a group composition against the sky. At any rate, birds can sometimes be arranged into a formal and stylized composition. The Normans entwined the long necks of swans to form corners on a manuscript page, and eagles have been transformed by medieval and modern American artists alike, into highly ornamental shapes. But, birds, too, look better in an individual composition than when they are manipulated into a repetitive formula, as if they were of the same nature as an acanthus leaf. Certain birds are symbols, of peace, of love, of hope, and this symbolic aura is articulated more clearly in one

tile than in the overstatement of many.

There was a time, in the seventeenth century, when Dutch tilers promoted a glorious vogue for light, sketchy renderings of birds, drawn in blue on white, with dabs of green and red to enhance feathers and sticks of foliage. These tiles were sometimes arranged in a wide panel with a different bird in each tile, the whole composition connected by motifs repeated on every corner.

English delftware of the same period also adopts a light and airy touch with little scenes of fishermen, houses, hunters, birds and beasts drawn in blue on white tiles. Both nations developed this very distinctive idiom: a sketch, a dot here, a dash there, a simple petal or a quick tulip on a slender stem, using blue on white. These artistic decorations are still a delight and look entirely right in a cottage kitchen, a period home or a modern apartment.

The Persians also have a store of bird images, rendered with a simple, graphic beauty. They have some lovely versions of the peacock whose strange, rich plumage is a perfect subject for ornament. The Art Nouveau craftsmen adored the peacock and produced an exhausting variety of images. The American Art Nouveau and Arts and Crafts movements ventured beyond the peacock more frequently than their European colleagues, creating some beautiful and clever compositions of rabbits or tortoises, often given a childlike quality which is very pleasing.

As we have already noticed, Victorian, and more modern, designs of birds and animals are painted onto tiles with less concern for their purely ornamental value. Tile designs then and now are more concerned to reproduce realistic and detailed images of animals and are not particularly interested in the design potential of animal subjects. What comes across is a trend for producing accurate representations of animals and an antipathy to the bold, stylized animal designs of Persia or the Arts and Crafts movements. Our choice of animal tiles then, is wide, varied, aesthetic and symbolic, with designs coming from every corner of the world and something to please everyone.

From the oceans of the world, there is the widest and most wonderful choice of naturally decorative and highly colourful creatures. Flat fish, starfish, octopus, pink salmon, pearly trout, playful dolphins, almost every fish is ornamental in shape and colour. There are some excellent images from medieval Europe and, again, the Japanese have made some of the most beautiful, clear-lined graphic designs of fish. Fishes become emblems which can be used freely in tiling, in kitchens and bathrooms, indoors and out.

Put it in Writing

Designers have long been absorbed by alphabets, scripts and the shape of letters. For centuries, words have been perceived as part of ornament.

Some alphabets are innately artistic. Little pictures of birds and boats and suchlike, were part of the Egyptian script, and the Chinese use brush strokes which are beautifully graphic in design. The graceful, swirling script of the Muslims is included in, or is the major part of, the ornament throughout the interior of a mosque, in the lintels over a door and in the domed roof. The lines of these letters are lovely and strange to most Westerners, but Muslims see not the design, but the messages 'Praise be given to God, the only one', or, 'There is no power or strength but in God' and other similar phrases. The use of Arabic calligraphy as ornament must be approached very carefully because to use such a message without belief in its meaning is profane. Perhaps we must forsake such ornament and simply sigh, as did a nineteenth-century gentleman: 'Ah, the good fortune of a people who can use an alphabet which is itself an ornament.'

The Celts loved to use letters as ornament, turning words round images and making letters into patterns. This, too, is quaint and attractive to our eyes, because few of us can read the letters easily, or understand their language. For this reason, Greek

CERAMIC PICTURES

Below Tile pictures, particularly at the turn of the century, were commissioned to decorate children's hospital wards. These designs often demand that words be included, as in the Cinderella story. *Royal Doulton Ltd.*

Trying on the Slipper

or Roman ornamental inscriptions are also acceptable for our use. Many of us do not know the languages and the script is merely decorative to our eyes. If we could read the words, the visual pleasure would be diminished and the ornament would transform into an archaic message, a forgotten name or an alien prayer. This is why calligraphy is a difficult element to include in our own ornament. Our own alphabet and our own language is not, for us, primarily decorative. It is the written word, and our minds register the message or phrase, causing us to think twice before including it as part of a design composition. Any words we use must be very simple, or very profound, in meaning. A message written in tiles on your kitchen wall may drive you mad if you have to read it every day as you stir a pot on the cooker! For instance, the quirky quotation, 'Comfort me with apples, for I am sick of love,' looks pleasing inscribed on a ceramic bowl and besides, you can cover the words by filling the bowl with apples! But if they were to meet your eye daily, in a tiled banner in the kitchen, you would be likely to fall into a philosophical decline!

Despite this problem, and despite the essential dullness of our alphabet, script *can* be used to pleasing decorative effect. The picture tiles in the children's ward at St Thomas's Hospital, London, not only showed scenes from *The Sleeping Beauty*, but also told the story in words inscribed on the tiles. The tiles for this fairy story were designed by Walter Crane and must have brought great pleasure to the ill children who were surrounded by them.

There is a lavatory in a library, also in London, which is tiled with the images and the limericks of Edward Lear. These decorated tiles are arranged amongst monochrome tiles and the whole effect is delightful, providing better reading than any magazine! It is a tiling idea that would work well in

ART AND COLOUR BOOKS

Left and below Tiles were frequently used as name plates and shop advertisements. some signs included words without pictures, a difficult design brief with our dull alphabet. *W. H. Smith.*

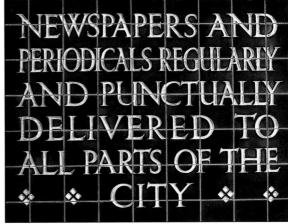

NEWSPAPERS AND PERIODICALS REGULARLY AND PUNCTUALLY DELIVERED TO ALL PARTS OF THE CITY

a children's bathroom or nursery and you need not use rhymes from Edward Lear, but, perhaps 'Mother Goose', or other nursery songs.

A tile panel with your street number written upon it and set in a gate post or beside the door jamb, is an attractive way of identifying your address, and children love to have their own rooms identified. A single tile, ornamented with a child's name and perhaps a little sketch of an animal or a bird, can be fitted onto a door.

But however hard we try we cannot pretend that words, whichever words we choose, will be simply ornamental. We read them, and thus their meaning dominates our senses.

Back to the Classics

The medieval scribes, stone masons and artists show us a world of naive charm, where ribbons of Gothic script weave round the figures of saints and heraldic beasts, who wander happily through the daily life of peasants feeding their chickens or sowing their crops. The unlikely juxtaposing of these various images assumes a validity because of the elegant linear style of the medievalists, but also because their work was full of a religious and symbolic significance. The most mundane event, such as an old lady pulling a thorn from her foot, two peasants flushing a bird from a bush, or even a serious battle scene featuring warriors in heavy armour besieging a castle, reveals an intensely pious world tied to the soil, the cycle of seasons, superstitious omens and, above all, the Church.

By 1500, this world was extinct. The manuscript scribes, those most patient and painstaking of craftsmen, who bent over their parchments

delicately decorating the words with little paintings and borders of gentle geometry and odd creatures, disappeared forever, crushed by the new technologies of printing, woodcut and engraving. Artists moved to the grander scale of oil painting and, indeed, the scale of art shifted completely. The pious symbolism was abandoned for a new aesthetic of humanism, stimulated by the ornament and subject of ancient Rome. An aesthetic code, unconstrained by religious symbolism but seeking 'beauty and truth', was to permeate the art of Europe. The era of the Renaissance had begun.

Renaissance ornament is a complex statement, combining realism with conceptual expressions.

The mix is one of classicism and ornamental effects and its intent is best described by F. Edward Hulme: 'Renaissance decoration requires, on the part of the designer, considerable knowledge, both of the kingdoms of nature and of the arts of antiquity . . . and calls for a mastery and power of drawing, plus a feeling for grace and a play for fancy . . .' So we find ornamental panels of goats and babies, drawn with remarkable accuracy but without consideration for their mutual proportions, entwined by scrolling leaves and scattered flowers; satyrs sport with nymphs, both entwined by garlands of ribbon.

Because ancient Rome and Greece were taken as models of perfection, Renaissance artists used the

key, the *anthemion,* the *guilloche* and other forms familiar to the ancients, and they made extensive use of scrollwork. Superb as Renaissance decorations are, they are not always suited to tile ornament. They sit beautifully on a page, or a fresco, on wrought ironwork or jewellery, but the taut grace of the line and the completeness of composition are not always compatible with the grid formation and diaper of tiles. This is ironic because the technology of ceramics had advanced considerably in Europe by the start of the sixteenth century. Information had filtered through from Moorish Spain and the other usual routes of war and trade via the Middle East. The Europeans learnt of tin-glazing and lustre ware. In Italy, a busy and inventive ceramic industry began to develop and a distinctive use of colour and technique emerged which was identified as maiolica ware (also called majolica).

The technology and colour palette were learnt from Islamic artists, but where Islam covered her buildings in ceramic tile and devized complex designs to decorate the tiling, the Italian potters saw the advanced technology as an opportunity to extend their craft into the area of painting. They were excited by the wide colour palette they could now achieve, and the fact that they could control the decoration with much more vigour than earlier ceramic methods which relied on stamping designs onto the clay. As Timothy Wilson says in *Ceramic Art of The Italian Renaissance,* 'The outcome was the extraordinary phenomenon of pottery treated as a form of pure painting, and the creation by 1510 of a fully narrative style. Unlike some forms of Renaissance art, *istoriato* ('story painted') pottery had no precedent in Greece or Rome . . . Under these circumstances some maiolica potters began to think of themselves as fully fledged artists in the Renaissance manner.'

These potters took to painting their dishes,

plates, jugs and mugs with pictorial scenes of Classical subjects – scenes from Ovid or dramatic episodes from Roman history. This *istoriato* work was in much demand, often to be displayed as *objets d'art* rather than actually used to eat off or drink from.

The colours used by these potter-painters were both subtle and strong – blue, green, orange, yellow, purple and brown, and, sometimes, an ornamental border encloses the painting in a frame, but, generally, Italian Renaissance maioloca is not a good source for the tiles we wish to use in our homes. We have to look to other areas, and perhaps the English Renaissance artists offer more – Inigo Jones, the Adams brothers, Grinling Gibbons and Josiah Wedgwood were masters in the decorative arts. But, even here, the distinctive Renaissance classicism is more suited to woodwork, plaster relief and book-binding, and these craftsmen do not offer a wide choice of design suitable to modern tiling use.

Dutch potters, too, were stimulated by the technology learnt from Islamic ceramicists but, unlike their Italian counterparts, they concentrated much of their skill on tile design. It was during this time that the distinctive Delft style, which remains popular even now, was first developed. These tiles carry sketches of daily life, drawn in a free, light manner. Separate scenes would be mounted into the tile grid, but a sense of ornament was achieved by the habit of decorating the corners of each tile with a reserve design. These were organized so that the tiles were placed against each other, the reserve designs met and created an ornament which served as a linking motif between the separate tiles, and gave a sense of repetitive unity to the tile grid. This is a very effective design trick and can easily be used if you want to create a tile area carrying numerous images of fruit, or animals, or flowers.

Another pleasing development in interior decorating was the decision to tile stoves and fireplaces. These Dutch fireplaces were known as 'smuigers' and they can still be found in the Netherlands, Scandinavia and parts of Germany. Here, the tile was demanded for its functional properties, and the designers were compelled to consider the use of the tiling and to ornament it accordingly. Homely scenes suited to the kitchen, connected by reserve designs, or held within repetitive borders, images of flora and fauna – all make charming tile decorations on these 'smuigers'.

But the Dutch potters were not immune to the possibilities of also being painters, and they developed an industry of pictorial tile scenes which were very popular. Large groupings of tiles carried biblical scenes, or landscapes, or great ornate floral ornaments. They were commissioned to create some extraordinary tile extravaganzas, such as the work ordered in 1716 by the Elector Maximilian Emmanuel of Bavaria for his Chinese pagoda at the Nymphenburg Palace. Here, 2,000 tiles were used to convey figurative, biblical and landscape scenes. But this excessive use of pictorial decoration, the turning of architectural ceramic into a debased mode of painting, was perhaps just another aspect of the Rococo style, which has been described as a 'state of bizarre chaos in the decorative arts'.

The Rococo era – the name comes from *'rocaille coquille'*, i.e. rock and shell work – was of French origin, and it certainly is an era of ornament run riot. However, as Rococo fell into fashionable disrepute, so the vogue for tiles in palaces, follies, shop fronts, dairies, kitchens and drawing rooms passed. The Dutch tile industry went into decline, and was only revived towards the end of the nineteenth century.

CHAPTER 3

Right Nature has been the design source for the ornament of both wall and floor tiles. A vertical line predominates on the wall decoration, but a circular theme has been used on the floor. However, these two elements are linked by a shared colour scheme. *Ruabon Tiles.*

The grand belief in Classicism, which created the beauty of Renaissance art, sustained all Europe for three hundred years. The principles of proportion and the rules of visual balance – the disciplines used to achieve an objective ideal of beauty – had given European artists an astonishing unity in their artistic and architectural thinking. But, as technology had vanquished the medieval world, so the beginning of industrialization and wider communication was to transform Renaissance Europe, that 'collection of societies composed of princes, peasants and corporate towns.'

Industrialization brought those peasants into the towns and cities and the power of the princes paled before the wealth of a new class of men. The structure and purpose of cities began to change, causing much confusion amongst architects and town-planners, but there were other developments which caused consternation in the world of decorative arts. Explorers and sailors were bringing back stories of other cultures that rivalled Classical Rome and current European achievements. Details of Indonesian and Hindu architecture, of Chinese temples and palaces, beautifully designed without any knowledge of the ancient principles of Greece or Rome, astounded Europe.

Artists travelled with these men who sailed about the unknown world and the etchings of their journeys were widely distributed. These revealed exotic plants, unheard of animals and birds and, even more exciting, the ornaments of strange tribes and peoples. Designers and craftsmen were entranced by the decoration and jewellery that these people had evolved and were fascinated to realize that forms of ornament familiar to Europe – the *key*, the scroll and other geometric formations — were also familiar to remote cultures all over the world.

Many were excited by the refined and beautiful artefacts of China and these were copied all over Europe, until the imitations developed into a bastard style labelled 'chinoiserie'.

Debates raged throughout the eighteenth century between the Classicists and those who argued for less rigid concepts of beauty, pleading for a wide and embracing tolerance of these new arts and ornament. These controversies would reach the height of eloquence in the nineteenth century, during the reign of Queen Victoria.

Gothic Victorians

In England, there had not been as strong an attachment to Classicism as there had been in continental Europe. England did not have many Roman remains to use as a model; grand ruins of marble did not loom up in the rural scenery, or grace the city corners; lovely cracked statues were not turned up by the plough. The English knew and were accustomed to their Gothic castles and cathedrals. The work of Inigo Jones and Sir Christopher Wren was admired but not widely emulated, and it was lost on most of the populace. Industrialization had come to England first; her cities were the first to be rendered ugly and sad by the fungus growth of slums. When the English turned their eyes to a more beautiful past, they saw their medieval heritage.

The Gothic style came to symbolize a better era and, once again, it was imbued with a religious significance. A man called Augustus Pugin voiced this emotional response and gave the pre-industrial yearning a shape and a purpose. He believed that if architecture and ornament returned to a truly Gothic character, not only the ugly cities, but the people themselves, would be redeemed. His was an intensely religious view and he believed that the

Roman Catholic Church, as it was structured in the medieval era, provided the only sane social system. He was convinced that the return of certain crafts connected with Gothic building would uplift the proletarian poor of industrialized Britain.

Pugin's ideas were to be expanded and expounded by John Ruskin, the Victorian art critic and historian, whose influence on his countrymen was considerable. Ruskin, contemplating the science of industry and the wonderful new machines that rescued the workers from hard labour, announced that 'Men were not intended to work with the accuracy of tools . . . If you will have that precision out of them, you must unhumanise them . . . it would be well if all of us were good handicraftsmen in some kind.'

Like Pugin, John Ruskin was ever a firm advocate of the Gothic style, with a similar belief that it made for an appropriate and uplifting environment. Ruskin approved of decoration, especially polychrome decoration (his favourite city in artistic terms was Venice) and the Gothic style allowed for this. The Gothic Revival in England did succeed in architectural terms, especially in the design of religious buildings and people's homes. The Classicists remained in the ascendancy in state and public building, but the turrets, towers and arches, the heavy ornament and decoration of Gothic, came to be synonymous with Victorian decoration. Perhaps Pugin and Ruskin did not intend this extravagance of ornamentation to develop, but then, both men underestimated the effects of mass production on popular taste.

The Artist-Craftsman

It is important to understand how technology and industrialization affected the artistic ethos in Europe. The Renaissance had caused a separation between artist and craftsman which was unknown to the medieval world. By the turn of the nineteenth century, the artists of Europe had assumed their own superiority over craftsman and, indeed, over most other people. This belief in the special superiority of the artist and his elite nature, was expressed by the English poet John Keats: 'O sweet fancy! let her loose; everything is spoilt by use.' The artist had begun to despise both the functional object and his public.

This artistic 'apartheid' led to one world of refined artistic sensibility and another of fumbling vulgarity, where inappropriate and very ugly designs were fed into the machines of mass production. The situation was revealed at the Great Exhibition of 1851, promoted by Prince Albert, husband of Victoria. It was mounted to display the wonders of industrialization, but uneducated manufacturers tried to reproduce, on their machines, the artefacts of the rich, and many unlovely objects were on display. Silverware was twisted and curled and heavily encrusted with enamelling; textiles were covered with 'copies from nature', which meant that unpleasantly realistic

Left and below The function of tiles is so well understood that the designer scarcely thinks about it, but concentrates instead on the decorative possibilities of tiles.

However, in this bathroom, the white tiled wall is a plain statement of function, but the clinical effect is softened by widely-placed individual tiles which carry floral ornaments.

Right A yearning for medieval beauty led Victorian architecture into a revival of the Gothic style. This led to a tremendous vogue for decorative tiles and the major British potteries produced pattern books for their customers. These sample designs show the popularity of floral ornament. *Royal Doulton Ltd.*

flowers covered carpets and curtains.

These incongruous designs were the statement of a people disrupted by an advancing technology, but it was the great English thinker and designer, William Morris, who perceived that the poor design and vulgar ornament of his contemporaries was also the result of that pernicious artistic 'apartheid'. Morris saw that artistic skill must not be confined to 'fine art', but that it should be generously applied to all objects, from the humblest pot to the grandest furniture. Artists ought to design the ordinary and not isolate themselves in their own esoteric world. Equally important to their artistic skill was a thorough understanding of the materials used to make everyday objects. Morris railed against the incongruous use of materials and ornament. He loathed coffee pots that resembled church turrets or ceramics used as paintings. William Morris cried, in direct contradiction to Keats and his ilk, 'What business have we with art at all, unless we can share it?' And for this we must remain ever grateful to Morris. He believed that everybody should live with good design, that it was the artist's duty to participate in the improvement of society. As Nikolaus Pevsner says, 'We owe it to him that an ordinary man's dwelling home has once more become a worthy object of the architect's thought, and a chair, a wallpaper or a vase, a worthy object of the artist's imagination.'

The Ornament of William Morris

In April 1861, William Morris issued a proclamation on behalf of his company '*Morris, Marshall, Faulkner & Company*: Fine Art Workmen in Painting, Carving, Furniture and the Metals'. Practising as preached, he launched his career as an artist-craftsman.

Morris was a superb designer, 'a master in the art

ENAMEL & UNDERGLAZED TILES.

H.

Nº 163.

Nº 337.

Nº 190.

Nº 184.

Nº 162.

Nº 139.

Nº 152.

Nº 77.

Right and below A random sample of Victorian tiles shows a wide-ranging and eclectic ornament. The coherent, flat floral forms, favoured by William Morris, appear next to bold graphics, influenced by Japanese design and realistic pictorial ornament of romantic scenes. *The Tile Collection, Royal Doulton Ltd.*

of enriching a surface'. He pursued the ancient and honourable habit of using nature as a design source, and, while keeping the recognizable shape of a plant, he abstracted the form into an ornamental design. The floral ornaments of William Morris are clear and sober, combined with an intense feeling for nature. We may be accustomed, now, to flowing floral designs, we may love them as chintz or dismiss them but, if we contrast them with the ornament of earlier Victorians, we begin to appreciate his more

Below Victorian experiments in technique and colour were encouraged by advances in technology. *Maiolica* glazes were developed, which gave a sheen to the ceramic surface. This was particularly effective on pressed relief work, and is still popular today. *Maria Rosenthal.*

rhythmical innovations of nature.

He turned to the regularity of form, the springing, growing lines of plants, and created designs of simple, strong convention. We recognize his chrysanthemum, daisy and grapevine, and we have a powerful aesthetic response to the imaginative order Morris imposed upon nature. He recognized the integrity of flat surfaces, and the constraints of the material and useage. He did not reproduce the shading and dimensions of real foliage, but created a coherent surface in his textile designs, which was both vital and flat. Morris favoured the diagonal meander: the twigs of his grapevine curl across the surface in pleasing curves and the indentations of his leaves are exaggerated to complement the meander; the diagonal of fruit branches is balanced by the straight, hanging weight of the pomegranate fruit. His designs catch the swing of movement, the push of growth which is characteristic of all plants, and his patterns are rich and close-knit, as foliage itself often is. And Morris had an instinctive awareness of the intent of ornament. His mastery of the decorative repetitive form achieved a coherent rhythm and no emphatic motif disturbs the eye of the observer.

He was careful to make his ornament appropriate not only to the qualities of wood, ceramic or textile, but also to the useage of the product. Thus, he rejected the diagonal meander on a ceiling paper and designed a flat duotone ornament with no direction, well suited to the visual effect of a ceiling. He designed and used furniture of a simple utility, enlivened by carved or painted decoration. Morris, the artist-craftsman, created a harmony between the material, the function and the ornament. He loathed the 'sham' techniques which controlled mass-produced objects, and the designers responsible for them.

But William Morris failed in one significant respect. His notions of art were fertilized by his own nostalgic anger and were nourished on his knowledge of medieval systems of work. He was unable to conceive that the artist would, one day, work *with* the machine, and he withdrew from the irrevocable industrialization of the world. He was to become *guru* to an earnest and vocal group of disciples who shared his ideas on the morally uplifting nature of craftwork, and on the integrity of the handcrafted object as opposed to the mass production of machinery. These were political ideas which led on to the social obligations of the artist and the ideology of socialism. His followers also listened carefully to his ideas on the coherence of material with design, his insistence on nature as the primary source of artistic principles and the relationship of artist to craft. These ideals were the foundation blocks of the English Arts and Crafts Movement and were to be carried all over Europe and the United States.

De Morgan – The Art Tiler

William Morris, inevitably, had designed for tiles, but his interest in ceramics was not as powerful as his passion for textiles and he did not pursue this line of design. He employed, and was closely associated with, William De Morgan.

De Morgan studied art at the Academy Schools and was motivated by Morris' social ideas on art and the artist. He began his working life as a designer of stained glass, but soon turned to ceramics. He loved the Iznik ware from Turkey, which he saw in the Victoria and Albert Museum, London (then called the South Kensington Museum) and experimented endlessly to repeat the purity and brilliance of their colours. He also admired Islamic ornament. The forms of nature, so beautifully expressed in these sixteenth-century Turkish tiles, were used and amplified by De Morgan. He took heed of William Morris' lesson that ornamental pattern work must show beauty, imagination and order, and that nature was the only legitimate source of inspiration. His designs are clearly related to the flora he studied. An appreciation for the arabesques and scrolls of Islamic ornament is conveyed in his regular arrangement of the pattern and the graceful geometry of his line. His designs have a graphic delicacy which create a rich ornament and De Morgan's tiles achieve a timeless beauty that allows them to decorate the most modern homes.

His tile designs were not restricted to Islamic-inspired ornament, for William De Morgan possessed a highly original imagination. He created some wonderful animal images, or, as they have been called, 'beasties', for many were mythical, or peculiar creations of his own. The Victoria and Albert Museum have a splendid series showing

Left Victorian visitors were given an aesthetic welcome, something to absorb their interest as they waited in the domestic entrance porch. Panels of ornamental tiles, decorated with floral designs or botanical studies, adorned the walls on each side of the front door.

Above The delicate symmetry of this tile ornament has been influenced by Islamic art. *The Tile Collection.*

Far left The functional aspect of tiling is not always significant. Collectors appreciate their decorative value, and arrange 'art' tiles to display their beauty, as in this panel.

Below This design reveals a mastery of decorative repetitive forms. Using nature as a design source, the lively movement of a growing plant is suggested in the rhythmical line and the flattened abstract forms of flowers and leaves.
The Tile Collection.

Right William De Morgan and his *guru*, William Morris, appreciated the tile as an architectural accessory, and promoted its use in domestic and public buildings. Hygienic and easy to maintain, tiles did become very popular in the nineteenth century restaurants, hotels and cafés. *H. & R. Johnson*

strange hedgehogs, sea-dragons, cranes and deer, interspersed with tiles of diagonally arranged foliage design. Other favourite subjects were ships, especially those of the classical trireme design, and single flower and bird impressions. De Morgan is a wonderful source of designs which can be considered for use in your own home.

He designed tiles for the Arab Hall at Lord Leighton's house in Holland Park Road and for Mr Charles Debenham's home in Addison Road, both London addresses. These were rich clients who could afford De Morgan's time-consuming and expensive hand-crafted techiques, yet both De Morgan and Morris longed to encase the homes of

ordinary men in tile sheathing. They believed that the functional value of tiles was perfectly suited to the dirty air of industrial cities, because the home-owner could simply hose down the tile façade and easily maintain the beauty of his property.

This was the dilemma of the Arts and Crafts Movement. The socialist principles of honourable craftwork for all, and art for all, were annulled by the expense of slow hand-made methods of production. Morris cried becaase he was catering for the 'swinish rich' and De Morgan, in order to earn a living, had to abandon ceramics for novel writing.

Art Nouveau Tiles

The artistic approach which William Morris had demonstrated was to be carried to its logical extreme by a generation of designers who came after him. His foliate ornament, analyzed from nature and structured to enrich a flat surface, now became an abstraction of natural form, flattened and curved into exaggeration by a short-lived but prolific movement of designers, whose work was called 'Art Nouveau' and which, to a greater and lesser extent, has remained popular up to the present day.

The movement was primarily concerned with the decorative arts. Where the Arts and Crafts Movement looked to a simple, sober return of the basic construction of furniture and household items, ornamented by forms from nature, or the medieval world (although as the movement gathered followers, the ornament tended to become romantically medieval or plain 'folksy'), the Art Nouveau designers preferred ornament for ornament's sake. Their furnishings and textiles were bizarre and luxurious in both shape and decoration.

They, too, used nature as their source, but the

Below This beautifully contrived design forms a coherent ornament on a single tile, but its rhythmical symmetry can also form a repetitive decoration in a multiple tile arrangement.

foliate forms were flattened and extended into trailing, unknown shapes, scrolled and curved beyond recognition.

Shapes became purely decorative and colour served to define one shape from the other, resulting in areas of brilliant, flat colour devoid of any tonality. The Art Nouveau designers were not concerned with the intrinsic texture of their material, but preferred to give a sinuous and sensual value not always compatible with the character of the medium. This disregard is demonstrated in their jewellery designs, where the metal support flows and softens over the stones, or in light fittings of inappropriate nymphs tossing light bulbs over their heads. And innumerable beds, sofas and chairs were rendered quite comfortless under wood bent

and curved into whirling arches.

The undulating, restless lines of Art Nouveau created a dubious form of ornament, but there are three areas where the style is apt and effective. Wrought iron, under an Art Nouveau designer, assumes a pliant, yet tense, decorative appeal, displaying the luxurious, graphic line with tactile strength. Secondly, the flat colour is transformed into glowing radiance when translated into stained glass, and, thirdly, the uninhibited tendrils and sprouts of organic life were contained to splendid effect by the controlled charm of the ceramic tile.

Art Nouveau designs were responsible for some of the most charming tiles produced in Europe and the United States. The swirling lines suit the texture of ceramic, as does the highly stylized foliate ornament so beloved by these artists. A rose, its petals flattened into harmonious ellipses, is supported on three symmetrical stems which flow into fat, shapely leaves – the colours are sugar pink and sharp green with black – and the whole design is contained in the tile rectangle. Yet the light, linear quality achieves an airiness and movement that extends the parameters of the borders. An iris is transformed into three petals of sweet curves, poised in a swirling line of foliage; a water-lily becomes a geometric design on an abstract wave of water. Each design is complete in itself, created

Far left A narrow format encloses an intricate ornament of numerous subtle colours, and reveals the craftsman's technical skill.

Left A sample group of tiles gives an example of the curved floral abstraction typical of Art Nouveau (top left). The Japanese use of pattern, instead of tonal shades has influenced the bird design. *The Tile Collection.*

Right Many nineteenth century designers favoured the 'painterly' qualities of realistic representations. These flower studies make a panel to decorate an entrance porch.

from neatly repeated curves of foliage which make a purely ornamental pattern of the plant. A whole line of tiles carrying the one design – of a rose, say, or an iris – will form a repetitive design motif, perfect for a border. Yet, just one tile of such a rose design will survive as a single, ornamental statement.

A few wonderful bird and animal images were created by Art Nouveau ceramicists. They were enchanted by Japanese design and the simple, strong forms achieved by the oriental artists. The flat, lineal quality of the Japanese style was a strong influence in shaping the Art Nouveau design ethos.

There are original Art Nouveau tiles still to be found in junk yards, antique shops, and tile shops which stock original tiles, and there are now many modern tile manufacturers who reproduce these delightful designs. The Art Nouveau style in ceramics retains a spruce air of modernity which appeals to our sense of ornament today.

Over the Top

The passionate promotion of beauty and ornament in every home, so strongly argued by William Morris and the Arts and Crafts Movement, led to a popular demand for interior design. This demand was fed by mass-production from the factories. The Arts and Crafts Movement had not reconciled itself to the machine, so its artists did not often submit designs to the industrialists, while the Art Nouveau designers were devoid of any political

Right This tile decoration recalls the work of Charles F. A. Voysey, who introduced delicate designs into an Edwardian market. *Eleanor Greeves Hand-Printed Tiles.*

Far right A modern bathroom achieves a 'period' feel with the use of Victorian style tiles. *H. & R. Johnson.*

or social motivations and tended to work for the rich and fashionable. At the start of the twentieth century, industrial design had not moved very far. As they always had done, manufacturers copied the current artistic vogue without comprehending its intent and, inevitably, the moral purpose behind Morris' work, together with the irrationalism of Art Nouveau, were both grossly misinterpreted.

Spiro Kostof describes the Late Victorian home: 'The absence of restraint was exalted as individuality. Bulk, clutter, conspicuous waste, these are negative readings for what were virtues to the Victorians – substantialness, variety, intricacy. They liked rooms densely thrown together, full of ornate furniture and bric-a-brac, framed maxims and prints of uplifting or sentimental subjects; gaily painted houses with irregular silhouettes, jutting elements and projections, crests, brackets, scrolls and finials; public monuments of stone and aggregates of curdled ornament.' This picture of Victorian architecture and ornament brings us closer to understanding the context in which Adolf Loos described decoration as a crime, and why the great American architect, Frank Lloyd Wright said quite firmly: 'Eliminate the decorator.' They were both appalled by the distortions they saw around them. The English, with their chracteristic sense of nostalgia,were trapped in a fey 'Gothic' ethos; in the United States of America, a thriving class of wealthy industrialists revelled in the ostentation of obvious and bulging ornament. But Loos, Wright, and numerous other architects and designers on both sides of the Atlantic, were evolving an architecture and ornament compatible, at last, with an industrialized world. They were to push popular taste into the Modern Movement.

The first tentative signs came from England. Charles F. A. Voysey (1857-1941) admitted to being a designer, but not a craftsman. He was not averse to employing men and machinery to realize his creative ends, but, more importantly, he was out of sympathy with the ornament of his time. His designs were radically different from those of Morris and his followers, who employed dense, closely-knit foliate curves, reminiscent of Islam and the medieval. Voysey preferred a delicate line in his rendering of simple leaf designs, and child-like images of animals which, while forming a repetitive pattern, were spacious and airy in their effect. Sir Ambrose Heal (1872-1959) followed Voysey's example and designed furniture of functional simplicity, with pure, geometric detail to serve as ornament.

Charles Rennie Mackintosh from Glasgow was designing buildings and interiors of astonishing

Below Avant-garde designers at the turn of the century insisted on minimal ornament and sought to create a sense of space. Modern taste has been strongly influenced by these ideas. The tiles in this bathroom use very little ornament and rely on sharp colour contrast for decoration. *Brausch & Co.*

severity, with an emphasis on vertical and horizontal lines. His ornamentation was subtle and elongated in form, revealing the geometry of his buildings. He used ornament to emphasize, balance and enhance, but not to obscure the spatial intentions of the architectural structure.

These three men shared a similar approach to design. In their work, as Nikolaus Pevsner states, 'there are no long curves; the patterns are composed of rectangles and gracefully drawn little flowers. The close atmosphere of medievalism has vanished.'

However, established tastes in England still reflected a more traditional view and, particularly in public or commercial buildings, the Classicist style persisted. Selfridges in Oxford Street, London, was built in 1908 and is a fine example of this neo-Classicist yearning, with its enormous columnular

façade and relief ornament. A truly innovative expression was to emerge from Europe and the United States from a generation that was not only reconciled to the machine, but wished to exploit it, to account for the machine-made in their designs. This generation was excited and stimulated by new materials and methods which offered the potential of evolving modern articulation congruous to the industrial world and the people of the twentieth century.

Eliminate the Decorator

The evolution of modernity was ruthless in its demands and ornament was an early victim of radical change. The decorated tile, the 'art' tile, found itself banished as ornament became not quite obsolete, but minimal. Architectural ceramics were employed for their functional quality and, when they were used, they were monochrome and unobtrusive. The primary aim of architects working before the First World War was to create space. They built with concrete, iron and steel, and these materials determined the line of the design. Buildings assumed an emphasis on horizontal and vertical structure, compatible with the shape and possibilities of the materials, and, also, architects preferred to expose the material rather than adorn it.

In Europe, there was a longing for space and utility. Architects such as the Austrian Adolf Loos (1870-1933), Otto Wagner (1841-1918), Josef Maria Olbrich (1867-1908), the French Auguste Perret (1874-1954) and the German Peter Behrens (1868-1940), were designing severely geometric unadorned buildings whose interiors relied on structure, not ornament, for visual pleasure. But it was America who produced a great visionary, the man who was to design a building of pure sculptural

Right Flower sketches in the 'peasant' style are fresh in colour and line. Individual-painted tiles are linked by a corner motif, a design solution learnt from the potters of delftware. *Rye Tiles.*

shape, the Guggenheim Museum, in New York. Even his early statements reveal a powerful sense of space and balance.

This man was Frank Lloyd Wright (1869-1959) and his was a profound individual mind which embraced all elements of design, to the extent that he specified every item and ornament in the interiors of his buildings. In his architecture, he conceived a wide geometric rhythm to express spatial freedom in which interiors flowed into exteriors, guided by long horizontal planes, supported, but not broken, by vertical supports. The quickest glance at Wright's work will reveal how very advanced was his vision; one has only to compare Heath House, Buffalo, New York (1905), the Frederick C. Robie House, Chicago (1906), Coonley House, Riverside, Illinois (1908) with the closed and monumental effect of the Selfridges building in London. Wright's architecture has a modernism which articulated exactly the appearance of future twentieth-century building design.

In his interiors, Frank Lloyd Wright maintained the harmonious, spatial flow. Furniture and fittings were part of a unified concept, and any clutter which disturbed the harmony was discouraged. If we look at the interior of the Edgar J. Kauffman House, generally known as 'Falling Water' (built at Bear Run, Pennsylvania), we see a perfect demonstration of the architect's approach to ornament. A room is panelled in a light wood. Fitting closely and unobtrusively, built in the same wood, are long angular cupboards. One cupboard carries, in the wood, a horizontal border patterned with a variation of Greek *key*. This motif is expanded and developed on one wall, again in wood, on wood. Geometric furniture, echoing the angles of cupboards and walls, is manufactured from the

wood. The upholstery and a rug are cream. There is no riot of colour, no jumble of shapes, no bulging ornament to disturb the calm spacious serenity of this interior. Stained glass was used to add colour and ornament in many of Wright's interiors, but here, too, there is a balanced use of colour and clear glass, expressed in sober, geometrical designs that utterly reject the fruity and ornate features of Late Victorian and Art Nouveau art glass.

The intelligent and radical spirit of Frank Lloyd Wright found a powerfully sympathetic response in Europe. He articulated an attitude to design which could have been the inspiration towards a new direction, a design technology which combined artist, engineer and the machine. He observed: 'Rightly used, the very curse machinery puts upon handicrafts should emancipate the artists from temptation to petty structural deceit and end this wearisome struggle to make things seem what they are not and never can be.' Frank Lloyd Wright expressed a growing and general dissatisfaction

Below Three different geometric forms are used on these tiled walls and the floor. The colours are so muted and the geometry so simple that the mixture of ornament is not awkward but complementary. *Ceramiche Cisa.*

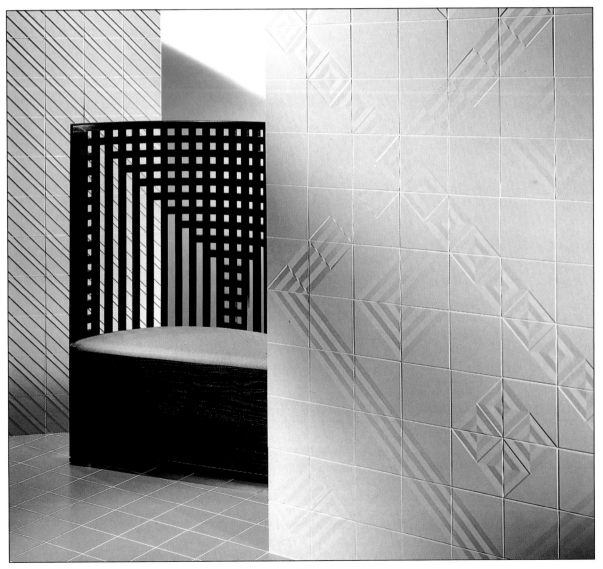

Below The sleek lines of these bathroom fittings are given a background of stark black and white. *Brausch & Co.*

Bauhaus and Others

At the *avant-garde* level ornament, and especially the decorated tile, languished in the first half of this century. The artistic *avant-garde*, who were superb publicists as well as being dynamic and imaginative, became absorbed in functional design to express political and ideological concepts. Starting with Le Corbusier (1887-1965) and centred on the Bauhaus School in Germany, grand plans were concocted for the perfect city, for utilitarian blocks to house, clothe and feed huge communities of workers. Design was severe, practical and minimal; the people were to be glad – or they must be persuaded to be glad – of the simple functional beauty of household items designed on strict utility lines. At the Bauhaus, which was led initially by Walter Gropius (1883-1969), students were taught a purely functional interpretation of the applied arts. They were expected to design and make textiles, household appliances and buildings, and were encouraged to work together to produce a proper democratic result, without individual eccentricities in their expression. (It is interesting to learn that the ceramics department at the Bauhaus was closed. The craft was too individual.)

Le Corbusier, the Swiss architect, was constantly devising housing schemes and city plans of efficient functionalism, but he also created some remarkable 'organic' architecture, which, while making full use of modern techniques, reverted to nature as a design source. His pilgrimage church of Notre-Dame-du-Haut in Ronchamp, France, has a widely curved, loosely tilted roof, balanced on leaning walls and assymetrical verticals. Le Corbusier claimed that the shell of a crab had inspired this design.

So much for the *avant-garde*. As ever, people outside the small band of taste-makers were using and demanding different models in their offices and

among young designers with the nostalgic backward view of the Arts and Crafts Movement and the extreme decoration of Art Nouveau.

In the decorative arts, designers now abandoned the obsolete hand processes and became fascinated by the certainty of machine-made products. Perfect clean lines and smooth surfaces were the characteristics offered by the machine and we see the growth of a neat simplicity in mass-produced items. Electric light fittings no longer pretend to be statues or ornamental objects, but are what they are: practical fixtures designed to express intelligently and clearly their household function. Coffee pots become containers with useful handles and easily managed lids.

Below This Art Deco ornament displays all the zany characteristics of the style with its mixture of curvilinear and rectangular lines, and disparate patterning. *Pipe Dreams*.

Right The minimalist design ideas of the Bauhaus School still exert a profound influence on modern designers. Subtle colours, combined with simple angular ornament on the tiles, give an effect of unbroken spaciousness to this bathroom. *Brausch & Co.*

homes. In the United States there was a frenzy of building, termed by Spiro Kostof as 'one of the biggest building booms in history'. Designs differed widely from the East Coast to the West Coast. In San Francisco and Los Angeles, designers turned to Spanish, Mexican and even Aztec motifs. Suburban homes along the East Coast sought refuge in resurrected neo-colonial styles. Industrialists were not pleased by the sternly functional and materialist approach of the modernists and demanded a livelier attitude to their commercial buildings.

During the twenties, before the Great Depression of 1929, a jazzy, colourful style of ornament was introduced in the form of Art Deco, deriving its name from the 'Exposition des Arts Décoratifs et Industriels', held in Paris in 1925. The Europeans tended to concentrate this style on objects and interior design, but not the Americans. 'In a short while, a whole repertory of angular and curvilinear forms was developed, none of it related to historical styles. Rendered in metal, terracotta or some other bright veneer, this ornament was woven into the exterior walls, spread out in entrances, lobbies and elevator areas, piled up into frothy confections for roof-top crestings. We can find these zestful Art Deco flourishes in the commercial buildings of most large cities – zig-zags, and dense floriate fields, faceted crystalline forms, stripings of various sorts, in glass and tile and mosaic and brass, often cheerfully juxtaposed.' (Kostof)

Elements of this zany mood of Art Deco can be transferred as ornament in modern homes, but it is essentially a 'style', a 'fashion'; and to achieve an authentic, recognizable Art Deco ornament, the whole room must carry the motif. This has to be done carefully and should be arranged with authentic contemporary furnishings and fittings. 'Reproduction Art Deco' is not a viable expression in the decoration of your home.

But the flat, stylized flower forms, rendered with a naive boldness, and the repetitive geometrical patterns can be utilized in tile decoration. There is also a positive Art Deco use of colour, a bold combination of clashing red with orange, blue with green, violet with yellow, which can be very interesting.

Designers now began to manipulate the decorative arts into expressions of vogue or fashion (they still do!) and when Art Deco reached its zenith, there was the 'streamlined' style ready to rush into its place. This was popular in the Thirties and 'streamlining' demanded curved walls, circular or rounded windows and a crisp, stark ornament. Brass and tubular metal was incorporated as ornament, and blacks and whites replaced the colourful gaiety of Art Deco. There is, however, an overlap between the two styles which results in 'streamlining' often being labelled 'Deco' in our own time.

There were also, during these fecund early years of the century, important developments in painting and sculpture. Totally original interpretations in imagery and form rocked the art world and, it must be admitted, aroused mockery and disbelief among the populace. Dadaists, Cubists, Picasso, Mondrian – some of these merely shocked, but other serious creative artists, chief among whom was the inimitable Picasso, wrought a profound change in visual perception. Such powerful statements from the painters was to affect designers and public taste alike. A sense of freedom entered the decorative arts, liberating them from historical reference and principles and allowing them fickle changes of expression.

In Our Time

The Bauhaus School, and others who wished to build a functional, modern world, promoted a standard of such pure utility and utter simplicity of form that it came to be called the International Style. These designers, had, in the manner of eighteenth-century artists, divorced themselves from the reality of the hum-drum, the sentimental and the eccentric in human life. When the Second World War was over, Europeans were shocked at the loss of some of their most valued historical landmarks, cathedrals, town halls, at the tragic despoliation of their cities. The tangible web of their culture, all that was familiar, loved and idiosyncratic in the architectural shape of their world, was in ruins.

No-one wanted to reconstruct with the bland perfection of the International Style. Indeed, Warsaw was rebuilt as it had been before the bombing, and French ports, like Nantes, were lovingly restored. Even the patina of ancient weather-worn walls was re-created. Human life needs its landmarks from the past, wants the haphazard but endearing forms of cities which have not been devised according to the smart and logical blue-prints of powerful, clever men.

The Americans, too, felt the loss of historic Europe and, with dismay, realized that devastation had been wrought in their own land by the busy, unheeding hand of developers and planners.

Architects began to display a more sensitive approach to the needs of the people who lived in the streets and buildings which they designed. They

Below Contemporary ornament is frequently defiant of traditional discipline and rules of design; it offers decoration that is haphazard in symmetry and colour combinations. However, the aesthetic pleasure to be found in precise, geometric shapes, as in these modern border tiles, has been enjoyed since the time of Ancient Egypt.
The Tile Collection.

Right This bathroom offers a stunning combination of triangle, diamond and rectangle forms in striking geometric designs.
Pipe Dreams.

grew more aware that a cosier scale than the modernists had visualized was the more comfortable mode for human life, and that brutal modern materials were not always able to express this scale.

The taste-makers were forced to look anew at their cities; they were compelled to leave grand ideological drawings behind and to observe that, mostly, their design dictums had been ignored or were irrelevant. Streets and buildings were not respected for pure functionalism; *au contraire*, they were densely ornamented with a slapdash vigour. Façades carried neon lights, billboards, advertisements – colourful, confused, large and vulgar devices which every twentieth-century city dweller understands, needs and creates. One American architect, Robert Venturi (b 1925), observed carefully and clearly and understood, as he contemplated the colour and bustle of the contemporary city, that architects must accommodate the facts of human activity. He wrote, 'The main justification of honky-tonk elements in architectural order is their very existence . . . these commonplace elements accommodate existing needs for variety and communication.'

Architects have since moved into a more difficult, but more satisfactory, situation of compromise. They must retain a regard for the historic, so dear to the people; they must maintain a modern sense of design, which does not disturb or quickly become irrelevant, and they must devise speedy, vital decoration.

The decorative arts have an easier role to play, although their penchant for the voguish can weaken their sense of balance and discrimination so that, in their eagerness to accommodate the vitality of the 'city scene', they have tried to reproduce the honky-tonk element' of the street within the calmer interiors of public buildings where such ornament immediately becomes incongruous.

But, for the individual, the personal home-maker, we live in an era of exhilarating liberty. Artistic taboos and principles of composition have been broken throughout our century, and we can achieve any ornament we wish in our own homes. Would William Morris, that stern old socialist, be glad that technology has given all of us this choice to have a beautifully ornamented home? Would he approve of our ceramic industry, which is both dynamic and capable of mass-producing a huge variety of designs for our own individual pleasure?

CHAPTER 4

Right Tiles can be used to make pictures, which decorate a wall with an effect similar to that of hanging a painting. This still life painted on tiles is even enclosed in a 'frame'.
Sylvia Robinson.

There is a wild licence in art and design in the contemporary scene. We have the choice, in our homes, to practise such licence, but this may not necessarily create a serene, harmonious dwelling place. There are forms and principles, developed for centuries since that very first amazing 'visual leap', which still guide us in organizing ornament to be aesthetically pleasing, and that give a foundation to all the endless design options which face the contemporary home-maker.

Tiles demand a certain discipline in their use, because they are laid in a grid; they are laid against walls and floors, and must accommodate the intrusive shapes of corners, cupboards, cookers and bookshelves. The ornament of tiles is related, ideally, to this geometric grid, and the majority of all geometrical ornament may be divided into three groups: bands or borders, which are continuous and ribbon-like, panels which are an enclosed, defined space, and there are unlimited flat panels. The groups can be mixed, which means that a subsidiary construction is introduced, or they can form a network. Keep these very basic concepts in mind when considering the ornamental intent of the tiles in your kitchen.

The contemporary ceramic market is a growth area, with consumers looking to improve the beauty and quality of their homes. In response to this growing need, the manufacturers offer a wonderfully varied range of tiles, both monochrome and decorated, in every and any colour anyone could wish for. There are modern designs which do not seem to follow a slavish trend, but are individual in seeking to please consumer needs, so that designs move from delicate floral sprays to bold abstract. Those countries which have a long tradition of ceramic tile making, Italy, Portugal, Mexico, Provencal France and Algeria, have also improved

Above The floral ornament of these tiles is based on the disciplined repetitive line and arabesque curves of traditional Islamic art.
The Tile Collection.

Right These tiles are based on an old peasant ornament. *Elon Tiles*.

their production, so that traditional peasant ornament can be part of our interiors.

The other delightful aspect of the advanced technology of ceramics is the ability to offer reproductions of ornament from every era of our cultural history. This makes a happy compromise for those wanting to restore a period home, and allows others to choose a design which otherwise may have been lost.

A dimension which our forefathers did not anticipate is the place of ceramic craftsmen in our highly industrialized world. Sustained by the demand from consumers which has caused the manufacturers to expand, these craftsmen supply those who want the unique and the special in their life. Also, despite the superb range and polish of manufactured tiles, the uncertain line made by the imperfect human hand at work, retains a profound charm and affection which the perfection of the machine cannot replace. We are fortunate that we can combine both methods of production in the ornament of our homes.

What Room?

The kitchen should be easily defined. This is the room where meals are prepared, but in many homes the kitchen assumes a significance, a value far beyond such a simple – and correct – definition.

This room is, in many ways, the heart of the family. Apart from furnishing the obvious appliances – the cooker, the fridge, the sink – it finds that it must accommodate a family calendar, where dental appointments and school football matches are recorded, notes from the school, naive posters for a jumble sale, a picture of the cat, then the dog bowl needs a space as does the cat's saucer, and the child's seedlings, tenderly watched as they sprout in cotton wool. In many homes, too, where space

Left Glimmering hues of muted colour in the tiled walls and work surfaces give a soothing background to a family kitchen. *Fired Earth.*

allows, the family likes to eat in the kitchen, or sit and talk to whoever's doing the cooking.

How to ornament such a room? Of course, when the first plans are made, the basic, essential kitchen confronts you. It has to be considered, primarily, as a room that is functional in a very real sense. There is no choice in the essential furniture. The cooker, the refrigerator and the sink have to be positioned and utensils have to be accommodated. Drawers and cupboards there have to be – food, china, glass, saucepans, vegetables, spices, sauces, must be stored. Some items can hang from hooks or be propped against shelves.

The kitchen is a workplace and the lay-out should offer maximum efficiency, minimum hassle. Certain appliances need to be near to each other, because they are so often used together. The work surface may look beautiful there, in that corner, but is there space for the mixer, the chopping knives, the stirring spoon? And is it not easier to store these in an open container within easy reach of the work surface?

And kitchen work has to be clean, carried out in a hygienic environment. This means that tiles will sheath walls where cooking fat, splashing sauces, sputtering oil land; tiles, of course, because they are quick and easy to clean, and extremely hard-wearing. For the same reasons, they seem the best and most practical solution to the demands of the kitchen floor. But, perhaps these uses for tiles are so obvious, that you need not pause to think of function – the delightful interest is the colour and ornament of these tiles in conjunction with the basic function and extended use of the kitchen.

You may perhaps look with aesthetic yearning at clinically neat kitchens that sparkle with hygienic efficiency, adorned in pale, cool colours, but, in your heart of hearts, is the certain knowledge that

Below Keen cooks are inclined to have cluttered kitchens. This busy collection of jars, weights, dry goods and the like are given a tranquil setting of rich-coloured monochrome tiles. *Rye Tiles.*

your kitchen is going to look quite different. When choosing your tiles and colours, think very carefully how you use this workroom. Do you like to keep your spatula, your wooden spoons, your draining spoon in a tall container, a jug, right by the work surface? Do you prefer your mixer permanently plugged in and instantly available so that it stands there, on the surface, where it is seen? Or does your temperament respond to artefacts being stored in cupboards and drawers when not in use? These considerations are very important when you are planning your decoration.

Tiles with an intricate floral design, an Iznik pattern, perhaps, from sixteenth-century Turkey, may be extremely pretty, and even soothing in their graceful arabesques. But when your kitchen utensils thrust themselves out of that jug and into the space backed by that intricate pattern, the juxtaposition of utensils and rich floral ornament will jar unpleasantly on the eye. The effect will not be soothing.

If yours is a kitchen that tends to be 'on the surface' rather than tucked away in storage areas, then a monochrome tiling will be more suitable. This will give your displayed utensils a certain visual value – even a positive visual value, if the container is chosen with consideration for your general colour scheme, and this container can be decorative to counterbalance the tiling.

Border Effects

A monochrome tile scheme can be decorated with a border design. Check whether the tiling area meets with hanging cupboards, before choosing a border. The conjunction may call for a bold ornament – a large scroll design that balances the angular line of the cupboard or, to emphasize angularity, a Greek *key*, or a simple rectangular

Below Traditional Norfolk Pammet floor tiles, with their charming irregularity of surface and colour tones, complement the carved wooden fittings of a rural kitchen. *Fired Earth.*

Below and bottom The colour combination of terracotta, cream and blue is infallible. It was used on Ancient Greek ceramic ware, and in their designs, too. The sample of tiles below is reminiscent of the sprightly line of Hellenic ornament. *Fired Earth.*

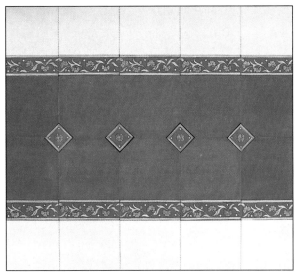

check design. A small delicate border will lose its significance if it is hidden in the right angle of the cupboard. Is the border intended to play an important decorative role in your kitchen? This may be the case if your other fittings are of basic geometric shape, but if you have chosen wooden fittings – which are themselves ornamental – with a carved wooden fret, or cupboard doors ending in curves and ornamental woodwork, the tile must complement, not fight, with the decorative shapes of the cupboards.

Another design solution for this family room-cum-kitchen is to use single decorative tiles plotted at careful intervals into the monochrome area. This allows the eye to rest briefly on a small decoration, but the visual effect does not become confused with the fittings or the appliances – or the activity of the room.

This is a family room, the heart-and-stomach of the home, where much love and energy is expended in the preparation of food – as such, the kitchen deserves, perhaps, symbolic ornament.

Private Symbols

We all have personal symbols in our lives – a certain scent arouses memories, tunes are associated with a person or event; the call of a bird, a flower, or certain animals remind us of security, of affection. We also share certain symbols with other people – a star or a cross of faith, the sign of the peace movement. Or we like the symbols other people use, and adapt them for our own use.

The Egyptian lotus symbolized life, or the giving of life, an apt symbol for a kitchen. There are charming variations of the Egyptian lotus produced on modern tiles and, if used discreetly – in a border, for example – a pleasing decorative effect can be achieved, without 'going Egyptian', and a subtle symbolic value is added to your ornament. A design

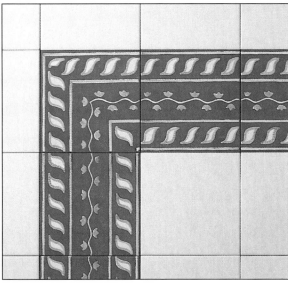

Left An oak kitchen is enhanced by the earthy, golden textures of antique French floor tiles. The wall tiles do not dominate in colour or ornament, but the white tiles do carry a border of Greek *guilloche* design. *Paris Ceramics.*

which represents a flow of life can be seen in a Cretan scroll, which is lively and rhythmical; or a *guilloche*, with its calm, round curves enclosing a flower shape, can express movement and flow. The Greek *guilloche* creates a large, firm border thus making a positive statement.

Animals and birds often carry symbolic value, and they are also a form of ornament which appeals to children. Craft tilers make some very charming animal and bird images, and it is worth spending the extra money on a few of these, which can then enhance your monochrome tile area. We all share the dove as an emblem of peace, and the fat, soft shape of a Picasso-type dove makes a marvellous ceramic ornament. Separate animal ornament as a repetitive row does not always – if ever – make for good visual effect, as has already been observed. To

purchase different sketches of the dove, one in-flight, one resting, is an obvious solution to this problem of repetition, but another is to create a little panel. Make a row of six images, or a square of four, and centre these into a monochrome surround. Or, if your tile surround has a delicate geometric or leafy ornament in duotone (if your doves are green, a green and white surround) this panel solution creates a focus, without over-stating the bird image.

Those Dutch potters in the seventeenth century loved to create a large tile panel of different birds on each tile, but this design demands a significant space in the same way as a painting does. To use tiles in this way, your kitchen would either have to be large enough to allow a special area – or small enough to make a major decorative statement of the panel.

Below, right and far right In the nineteenth century, the Arts and Crafts Movement emerged as a reaction against the growth of factories and technology. The Movement's followers feared that handicrafts would become obsolete. Yet, despite the highly-efficient and productive technology that exists now, individual craftsmen are still working. *Exim Group; Criterion Tiles Ltd.*

The range of floral ornament on tiles is enormous, and choice ranges over centuries and centuries of artists' drawings of flowers. The designs vary from the unsuitably realistic, to beautifully conceived rhythmic designs, or graceful little 'folk' sketches from Provence, Mexico or North Africa. The way to define your own range of preferences is to look for the species of flower you like most, or that which symbolizes something for you. Also, of course, there is an endless variety of designs – flowers placed diagonally, in circles, in curves, in star shapes, alternated with monochrome tiles. This is an area of ornament that is bewildering in its choice, and the best advice is to make your own symbolic-aesthetic choice. Try and avoid those unpleasant 'realistic' images, for they do not make good ornament.

Small Kitchens

Many modern apartments and town houses do not make any concession to the notion of a kitchen serving an extended purpose. The designers create small, neat spaces dedicated solely to the business of preparing meals. (Some designers are even reluctant to allow storage space!). The tightly-planned functional space demands brisk, efficient use. The tile ornament can be used to emphasize this. An angular, geometric design makes the correct statement. Quite often, with very small kitchens, there is no space for any other ornament, or the clutter of calendars, chairs, pretty jugs or the like, and the tiling is the only decorative element. As such, it can be used boldly. Is one wall blank, facing a galley work area? Tile it from ceiling to base and make a great bold zig-zag swing from top to

Left Modern hand-painted tiles are shown in situ in a kitchen. *Ceramiche Cisa.*

bottom, or a diagonal stripe from corner to corner. The use of Art Deco shape and colour could make this very striking.

A bold border design, however, is not a good design solution for a small area. The border will reduce the sense of space and, because it forms horizontal and/or vertical lines, the little kitchen will be cut up into cubes. Single ornamental tiles plotted into a monochrome surround will suit the space better than a border, and better than an overall repetitive design which will reduce the visual spatial effect.

Some may find the essentially utilitarian aspect of a small kitchen daunting or depressing. A frivolous ornament will take care of the problem. The delicate flower sketches, or little rural scenes, so typical of delftware , the bright, airy flower tiles of Algeria or Mexico, or 'beasties' in the De Morgan style will all serve to counteract the stern functionalism. But keep the ornament spruce and spare so that the confined space is not rendered oppressive.

Colour Content

Because the decoration of tiles is so significant, it is essential to understand what the intent of the ornament is. Does it say what you mean it to say? Does a rhythmic scroll, or an angular chevron, suit you and your kitchen? Are flowers or birds appropriate? Are you certain that this is the ornament you want, or is it a passing 'style' of which you will tire in a few years? And, perhaps, the ornamental line is not as significant to you as colour is.

Below A bold background of deep blue tiles, bordered by a band of golden orange, emphasizes the bulky stove in an otherwise monochrome decoration.
Fired Earth.

There is a tradition of cool colours in kitchens – white, or blue and white, creams, beiges. Perhaps this was to counteract the heat of old-time cooking stoves! Now, however, there are bold kitchen designs and bold use of colour. There is a solid, gleaming red which modern manufacture produces; so rich in hue, that it needs to be combined with black and grey as white would be too sharp a contrast. It achieves an effect of dense warmth, and works in a very small kitchen, or in one area of a large kitchen – near the breakfast bar, or surrounding the cooking area. Such a hard, brilliant colour demands an emotional response, so it should be used with care. Red is also a colour which carries many connotations: it spells grandeur, it symbolizes passion, and it has a certain disreputable quality (Paint the town red!). Think what statement you wish to make with red.

In contrast to this hard, enamelled colour tone, there is a range of gentle, shimmering hues – pastels of blue, or of pink, or of creams. These soft hues do not carry a wall covering easily, but graduations of tone – icy blue, dusty blue, sky blue – look well as work surface, or on a deep window ledge. Here, the eye can wander over the colours and then leave them, but on the wall they demand a slightly sentimental attention. Used on a work surface, they look best set against a creamy white tiled wall, and the sweet effect can be sharpened by the use of tile border designs. Where the surface meets the wall, place a single row of clear blue ornamented tiles, and repeat this at the top edge of the wall tiles. Keep the ornament small and unobtrusive so that is serves to sharpen, but not overwhelm the soft shimmer. (These 'shimmering' colours are glazed, and come from France.)

Left Here, monochrome and ornamented tiles are arranged to make obtrusive, but essential fittings into an integral part of the room's decoration. *Fired Earth*.

Above Victorian-type relief fruit ornaments can be seen on a sample panel. *The Tile Collection*.

Left Blue sketches, in the Delftware style, with each individual study on its own tile, decorate this sink surround and complement the tiled work surface. *Elon Tiles*.

Below The tough quality of ceramic tiles makes them an appropriate work surface. In this kitchen the tiles are decorated in a brightly coloured ornament of a Spanish style, and the 'peasant' look combines perfectly with the terracotta floor tiles. *Elon Tiles.*

Below right The hi-tech fittings of the kitchen are quite at ease with the shining green Victorian *maiolica* tile surface, and the pressed tile relief ornament. *A. Bell & Co. Ltd.*

If pastels are too insipid for you, green is well-suited to a kitchen. It has inherent qualities of freshness and cleanness, reminiscent of foliage, grass and meadows, and, yet, retains a warmth. It also sits well with other colours – with yellow, with red, black and white. Kitchen tiles bearing a green ornament, something with an intricate line such as the Greek *anthemion* or a complex *key* or diagonal, can achieve a stunning effect. It is not a demanding colour, which is why it can carry a complex line, and it gives an exhilarating touch to a functional room.

The Islamic ceramicists used delicious bright blues and greens, and, although these colours do not work used as a major colour theme in the kitchen, they do offer a cheerful and rich display in tiling borders. Other startling colour combinations can be found in Art Deco ornament but, again, such richness is not advised as a major element. Keep the Art Deco red/orange to a thick zig-zag border. This is not to dissuade anyone from the use of daring colour usage. But the intent must be understood. The Scottish architect, Charles Rennie Mackintosh decorated some interiors in mauve, rose, bright green, black and white. The reaction is to scream,

Left This sample shows hand-painted tiles with the charm of imperfection which is the mark of the human hand and is so different from the results achieved by machinery.
The Tile Collection.

'But not in the kitchen!' But why not? If the walls and fittings are kept white and the appliances black and white, then a bold floral ornament of mauve, rose and green, preferably in the undulating lines of Art Nouveau, would present a stunning contrast. These border colours could be repeated in odd details – green door knobs, a green kettle, or a great rose fruit bowl. Such colour usage and ornament is a very positive statement of stylistic intent, and does not allow for clutter, or for the use of other colours in the kitchen.

Colour is a wonderful 'maker' of atmosphere, but it does drastically affect the spatial qualities of a room. A kitchen carries, perforce, many fixtures and fittings which can absorb space. Your main colour theme must retain or expand this space, not lessen it. Again, the traditional blue and white do not intrude on the kitchen. Colour is best expressed in a lyrical and decorative tile ornament rather than in the use of a powerful overall colour. This is the joy of ornamental or 'art' tiles, for they permit intense points of colour in a way that cannot be achieved by any other decorative device in the kitchen.

White on White

This is a difficult design approach in kitchens, but it is not impossible to make it work. There are some magical pearly whites achieved through a process called iridescent glaze. The Islamic and Victorian ceramicists loved the varnished brilliance which iridescence achieved. Used on white tiles, it glows rather than shines. It does create the almost-pastel shades of mother-of-pearl when used on white, but this is probably too romantic for a kitchen. A white kitchen has a determinedly surgical look, and should be reserved for that small functional space which is the apartment kitchen. Used in a big room, it would create a glaring and unwelcoming effect

Below The monochrome tiled walls are broken by a panel of floral ornament which has been placed to give the functional cooker a decorative quality. *Elon Tiles.*

and would have to be counterbalanced with work surface tiles in colour, and a strong, colourful border, which means, of course, that this is no longer a white kitchen. Keep white for a tiny kitchen, and those romantic mother-of-pearl hues for a bathroom.

Textures and Tiles

The kitchen does not come made to a standard design, even if many of its appliances do. There are styles and moods, created by the shape, the light and the materials employed. These should be combined into a harmonious whole, and tiles play an important part in the planning process.

A country cottage look may suit a certain type of room. Open brick-work surrounds an arched cooking area; cupboards, sink stand, doors and windows in golden-hued or old dark wood contribute to this positive design element. It would be incongruous to introduce a harsh bright Art Deco ornament or a chic geometric black and white design into this country atmosphere. Also, in an old country kitchen, there may be large windows allowing plenty of natural light. Jazzy tiling will only look tawdry. Choose quarry tiles, or tiles of a terracotta appearance; tone down colours – use thick cream rather than brilliant white, and choose a motif that reflects the old and the rural such as an ivy-leaf design, which is curved and gentle. Again, use muted colour hues in the border ornament and, if the terracotta look is chosen, complement it with a simple line of colour rather than a bold and bulky design to distinguish any ornament.

An apartment kitchen may have very limited natural light; electric light is significant here, and, anyway, a hi-tech decor has generally been fitted. Smooth, gleaming surfaces of white, picked out with

Left Muted pastel tones used on the cupboards and walls allow the warm honey tones of the terracotta floor tiles to dominate. *Castelnau Tiles.*

Above The shimmering colours of the tiled work surface give a decorative note to the neat efficiency of this kitchen area. *Fired Earth.*

Left The special qualities of a kitchen which is used for eating and relaxation, as well as for cooking, are expressed in the comfortable, warm tones of antique French floor tiles. *Paris Ceramics.*

Right Terracotta floor tiles can be placed so that varied patterns are created. This example shows the use of small diamond-shaped link tiles, some of which carry decoration. *Elon Tiles.*

Far right The rich, earthy tones of the terracotta floor offsets the cooler effect of the blue and beige tiles above the work-surface. *Paris Ceramics.*

shining black rails and handles, the cupboard doors made from a subtle grey matt material; obviously, terracotta peasant tiles would look absurd. But, then, so would soft delicate flowers, or quaint little bird images. The hi-tech quality would be disturbed by colour touches. Here, too, the hard enamelled red would be too brutal a contrast. Gleaming white, or shining black tiles, or perhaps an enamelled navy, but tile usage must be simple, subtle and clever if it is to remain unobtrusive.

Many of us have converted kitchens from what were once dingy storerooms or old wine cellars. The walls have retained their roughness, but they are whitewashed. This style of kitchen needs a perkiness, a cheery note to take it far away from its inadequate shape, or basement atmosphere. Here, use the lovely Mexican flower designs – dense clusters of naive daisies, or marigolds, connected by reserve designs in the corner, or forming a diagonal ornament with alternate tiles of a bright monochrome. With tile ornament of this nature, the essential 'rough' texture of the conversion is brightened by uncontrived but colourful decoration. Smooth, slippery colours would only make a statement of unbecoming sophistication.

And the Floors?

A truly extraordinary range of floor tiles is available to us. Look, for example, at terracotta, and you will discover that there is no such thing as a simple terracotta floor. There are wonderful rich red-browns with a pitted texture; there are red-brick tiles made to Roman specifications; there are mellow orange hues, black with ox-blood, mushroom-coloured rectangles, honey-hued hexagonals; there are squares, octagonals, diamonds, borders and insets.

The remarkable characteristic of all these tiles is

Right and below right Most
kitchens are crowded with cookers,
kettles, containers and all the other
paraphernalia associated with the
storage, preparation and cooking of
food. The floor, the base setting to
the essential 'busy-ness' of this
room, needs to be functional, durable and unobtrusive. Yet these
sensible qualities do not mean that
floor tiles are dull. The range of
colour, texture and ornament
available which fulfils all practical
needs, yet offers aesthetic pleasure,
is enormous. *Paris Ceramics;
Korzilius Söhne (Barbee Ceramics).*

that they are functional in colour and shape,
unobtrusive in tone, and can be used in kitchens of
the most varied colour schemes, ornament and
mood. The colour range of these terracotta tiles is
subtle, but the deep hues would look best with reds
and navies, the honey with greens and yellows, the
mushroom rectangles with pastel and clear, light
colours. But this is mere quibbling.

The decorative value of terracotta tiles relies on
the pattern in which they are laid. They can be
formed in a chevron if they are rectangular; squares
can be turned to diamonds, octagonals are
interspersed with tiny diamond fittings. The laying

of these floor tiles is based on those principles which
the English medieval tilers followed, and which are
described in an earlier chapter. The laying can
incorporate various patterns, so that the outer edges
are in straight stripes, but a diagonal enlivens the
central area or a chevron surrounds a separate work
unit in the middle of the room.

Roman and Greek ornament is being reproduced
in terracotta tiles, so this can be used to enliven the
floor or to separate the area between the straight
stripe/diamond laid tiles.

From Mexico a splendid range of glazed 'pavers'
comes in colours beyond the terracotta range. Ivy
greens, gold, beige, blue, grey – these can be used as
a monochrome surface, or alternated – gold with
blue, or ivy with grey – in diamond patterns or in
stripes. There is an infinite variety of geometric and
colour combinations. These Mexican tiles are highly
compatible with hi-tech kitchens, or that basement
conversion which needs a luxurious touch.

The Symbolic Space

A kitchen, no matter how functional the designer
makes it, no matter how neat and 'Bauhaus' its
appearance and its appliances, serves a profounder
purpose than simply the preparation and storage of
food, yet it is food that alters the function of the
kitchen.

The sensual pleasure of the essential; the care and
the thought and the love that is poured into the
preparation, the delight, the joy in the eating; all
these emotions flow in the kitchen.

It is a place that must express and reveal these
essential pleasures; it must be a place that is good to
be in. The ceramic tile is a material that carries dual
qualities – those of function and of beauty. Choose
your kitchen tile ornament with due care – and a
sense of enjoyment.

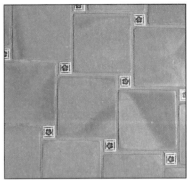

Below and far left The samples here are handmade terracotta tiles from England, Europe and South America. *Castelnau Tiles*.

CHAPTER 5

Above Subjects and symbols which suit the bathroom can be subtle and witty. The surrealist artist, Salvador Dali, designed a starfish on a ceramic tile – a subject that instantly announces a watery element. *Fired Earth*.

Far right In this bathroom the border tile ornament is less easily recognized for its watery associations, for it carries a conceptual shell design. *Pipe Dreams*.

Bathrooms are very new; within living memory there were millions of homes in Europe and North America that did not have indoor plumbing and a bath. Nowadays, few homes are deprived of this important room, but many of us still regard the bathroom as a luxury area, deserving of glamorous fittings and ornament.

There are so many superb tiles available to enhance the pleasure and luxury we seem to attribute to the bathroom – not to mention the variety of coloured baths, streamlined taps, shower fittings and improved toilet shapes – that we are faced with a bewildering number of options when choosing our design scheme.

Because water is the important element here, we can start our quest for ornamented tiles among the many quirky symbols associated with it. There are shells and waves, octopus and fishes, mermaids and goddesses, and even seaweed. There are aquatic colours – clear blue, aquamarine, grey, navy, pastel blue, ice cream blue, white, mauve, green – symbols all. But what of the aesthetic qualities? What do we *need* from our bathrooms?

Water Sign

The ancient Minoans gave us the earliest and the best models of design inspired by the sea, but there are other offerings, including some from Salvador Dali, who created a lively tile design with a starfish of red on yellow. For those who favour images of creatures, there is a choice of the mythological, the colourful, the bizarre to be found amongst those that inhabit the sea.

On Greek boats even now are painted playful mermaids. Their yellow hair streams in waves from their little faces and runs parallel over a long and curly blue-scaled tail. This is a witty, happy image, and can be put to good use, in a light-hearted

Right Mythological creatures of the sea romp across these tiles and make a quaint ornament for the bathroom. They are obviously associated with water, but, in the floral design below them, the sun and sea are evoked by the colours not the subject. *The Tile Collection.*

Far right Subjects from the sea are represented in these pressed-relief tiles. *Maria Rosenthal.*

bathroom. Make a small four-square panel, so that four merry mermaids entertain you over the bath. Turn back to the seventeenth century and serious, wistful mermaids in monochrome can be found, but these will not suit a panel; rather plot three or four into the diaper of the tiles. A pink mermaid printed on a white background, and placed into a pink tile grid will create a fey and romantic ornament.

The Minoans played with the scroll; they curled the line inwards, they flicked it upwards. Whichever way it is used, the scroll can serve as a modern symbol for the sea. Make a blue border of a scroll design, which is not only attractive, but serves as a curvaceous contrast to the angularity of the bathroom fittings.

The sea horse and the octopus are not obviously symbolic, but they have intrinsically ornamental shapes and many designers have rendered their fascinating forms in a hundred different ways. Dolphins, too, have a line and movement that translates naturally to a design format. In fact, dolphins are one of the few living creatures that can be transformed into a repetitive pattern, if used as a very small ornament. If symbolism and significance are what you are seeking in your bathroom ornament, there are birds which are associated with water – not just the sea birds, in formation.

Other Sea Designs

A favourite and artistically fascinating study for desingers is the sea-shell. The sea-shell! There are *thousands* of different sea-shells, all with curving, spiral forms, many with strange interesting markings. The shell can be used as a repetitive pattern, or as one unique image in your bathroom

design, and this ornament allows any choice of colour, without losing its association with the sea.

There are bathroom fittings which echo the pattern of shells – the basin curves with the shape of an oyster shell, as does the bidet. I am not convinced that this needs a tile ornament, or indeed any other ornament at all!

There are some marvellous abstract renderings of water, or the sea. Look back to the Egyptians who, with three rows of gently waving parallel lines indicate the movement of water with perfect economy. The familiar old zig-zag has been turned to good use as well, lying beneath a fish or an octopus to illustrate their watery environment.

Below left The scroll, that Minoan symbol of the wave, is used to ornament a tile border. *The Tile Collection*.

Below Shimmering, reflective green tiles create a watery surround to this small wash area. *Margery Clinton*.

Below The purity of function, without embellishment of ornament, unmarked by colour, is the design approach used in this bathroom. The tiles create a visual interest with their geometric relief, but the smooth hygiene of the tile surface predominates. *Ceramiche Cisa.*

Colours of Water

The sparkle of foam, the milky white froth of bubbles along a beach, the white glare of sea sand, the bluish white of the horizon. These are the whites of water. Of course , a prosaic reason for the use of white in the bathroom is because white is closely associated with cleanliness, but combine the two ideas and use the hygienic white romantically. This is the moment to choose those shimmering soft white tiles of iridescent glaze, the mother-of-pearl, almost-pastel, white.

This particular glazed white does not need another colour for emphasis or contrast. A second colour would diminish the subtle sheen to a mere background. Use only mother-of-pearl tiles, but pattern the tile grid. Set one row as diagonals or diamonds, or make a star shape. A narrow border, indented or in relief but with no colour, accompanies this tile. The hard white of the bath and basin fittings may also detract from the total effect; choose instead a very slight blue-white or pink-white for these fittings.

There are many shades and hues of blue if the watery image is to be followed into colour, but always remember that the tiles have to surround the obtrusive jutting shapes of bath, basin and lavatory. Choose a colour or hue that complements the fittings and does not push them further out into the room.

Modern tiles can create the entire ornament of the bathroom and, if the room is big, the designer has scope to arrange a grand geometry of gleaming, articulate stripes or diagonals that cover the bath, the floor, the walls – a total concept in the tiling of the bathroom.

Practicalities

Like the kitchen, the bathroom and shower area

Left A concession to decoration has been made in this bathroom of hi-tech fittings which are relieved by muted floral tile ornament. *Bernard J. Arnull.*

Below The painted floral panel is an example of a more traditional and rich ornament. *Lambeth Tiles.*

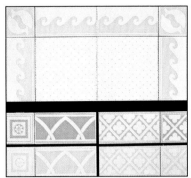

Above Sample tiles of subdued colour and geometric design would suit an emphatically functional approach to bathroom design. *The Tile Collection.*

Right Bathrooms, like kitchens, are essentially functional. Monochrome tiles give a calm background to fittings and utensils, but can be enlivened by a scattering of quirky, sketched tiles. *Fired Earth.*

must be kept clean, and as tiles are super-easy to clean, it is practical to use them. But there are many accessories to be kept in the bathroom – shampoo bottles, soap dishes, toothbrushes, tooth mugs, toothpaste, backbrushes and flannels, perfumes, nail-clippers, talc, cotton wool, and probably the family medicine chest. And towels, and shower caps, and lavatory paper, and shaving gear.

Some of these items will be stored in cupboards, some will stand on shelving, some will cluster round the basin or the bath, depending on where their most frequent use is found. All these things are taken into account with the right fittings, but frequently, as in kitchens, the way things are used is not taken into account. Like the modern architects who looked out of their windows, and noticed that they had forgotten to account for the 'honky-tonk' existence of the people who were using their streamlined buildings, so, too often, do designers neglect to arrange a room so that it suits the users, not the decor.

A beautiful ornament of tiling will be destroyed by wet towels hanging in front of it or a cluster of shampoo bottles on the side of the bath. The decoration of the tiles must not jumble up with the usage; the usage must be considered, and the ornament designed to suit that.

If the bathroom is used by the entire family, the number of people and their individual requirements must be understood if the tile ornament is to have any aesthetic value whatsoever. It is safe to assume that most families will need a sense of space in their bathrooms, not a feeling of confusion, and, if this is the case, a simple border on monochrome tiling is the best ornament.

Boudoir Bathrooms

There is a dreamy approach for those bathrooms that call for a soft, romantic ornament. Here, water is not the prime concern, and all those symbols of the sea, the colours of blue, are irrelevant. The boudoir bathroom is soft and feminine; it is a place of perfumes and scented sprays and aromatic soaps. It is a centre of luxury and self-indulgence.

Dreamy colours would demonstrate this idea of the bathroom. Iridescent glazes, those shimmering pastel hues in soft pink, muted mauves or thick cream tones express gentle relaxation. The indulgent curves and swirling lines of Art Nouveau, with its extensive use of floral forms, express a sense of luxury, although there are other sources of romantic ornament. The Romans used a slow easy scroll which encompassed a leafy form, and some of the Renaissance and Islamic curves would also make the right poetic statement. Do not let the ornament be too loose, or overstate the romantic, because the effect will become sentimental, not sensitive. Introduce an element of acid – a sharp green in the Art Nouveau ornament, or

Left A decorative corner will compensate for monochrome tiled walls in the rest of the bathroom. *Elon Tiles.*

Above Coloured tiles, designed in a flowing 'peasant' fashion, suit such concentrated use of ornament. *Carmona Tiles.*

Left The severity of tiles placed diamond fashion on walls and floor are another solution to counteract the clutter of the family bathroom. *Fired Earth.*

Below A panel of decorative tiles, based on ancient designs. *The Tile Collection.*

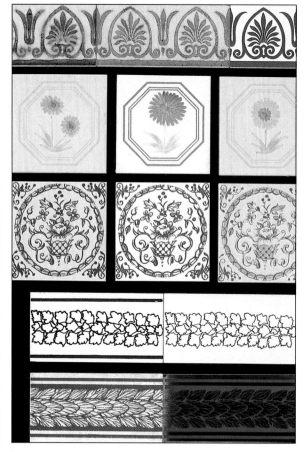

Right The use of a band of individually decorated tiles is a clever substitute for the more usual border of repetitive designs. *Rye Tiles.*

incorportate a very thin black line in the curvaceous floral pattern.

Without Sunlight

Numerous conversions or refurbishments of enormous private homes into a series of private apartments, have produced architectural solutions that allow rooms to have no window. For instance, what was once a pantry becomes a bathroom, or the corner of one large drawing room is divided off to create a shower or bathing area. This lack of natural light will affect any decorative decisions.

Electricity sheds a harsh light and although this can be, and usually is, controlled by shades, bathrooms do require a brighter light than most other rooms. Consider how harsh light falls on the colour of your tiling. Modern ceramic tiles generally have a smooth, gleaming surface, and tend to glitter under electricity. White tiles, for this reason, can actually become relentlessly harsh in their effect. Soft colour, or muted pearly whites, are the correct design solution to this problem; or a joyously polychrome border can relieve the stern glare. Or one can reduce the tiled area to a minimum, so that the less reflective wall surface absorbs the light.

You may choose to emphasize the glitter of white with chrome or stainless steel fittings, a white floor, white ceiling, and so achieve a highly clinical, super-hygienic and purely functional bathroom. No boudoir romance or watery environment in this sternly practical bathroom. (But do not expect children to appreciate this particular approach.)

Bathtime

Children go through phases of loving the bath, or hating the cleaning process. A cheerful bathroom, designed for their pleasure, can help bring about that happy attitude which perceives bathtime as

playtime.

Clear, bright colours – an apple green, shining red, or red and white – can be relied on to attract a child's attention, and witty tile ornament will arouse interest. Sea-horse emblems or spotted fish, endearing cartoon animals or the naive rendering of medieval cats, dogs and birds, will be appreciated. Plot individual tile images into the tile grid so that the restless eye can contemplate a duck here, a swan there, a goose in the corner. A colourful and complex border ornament, set in the row where tiled wall meets bath is close enough for a small finger to trace the curious design, and is therefore tailormade to suit a child's bathroom. Such a border is not always a good design technique because it can

Right The use of fully tiled walls is very functional, with little ornament, but the bold red monochrome elevates this practical statement. *Exim Group.*

Below A rich decorative effect achieved with glimmering tiles. *Margery Clinton.*

divide space too roughly and give undue prominence to the bath; but a child's bathroom shouldn't be subject to adult rules, and can carry a 'cluttered' effect.

Because the hardy tile is quite difficult to remove once it is fixed on the wall, choose ornament for the children's bathroom with strong aesthetic considerations. Children do grow up, and if their bathroom is tiled with charming Edward Lear limericks or drawings, or cleverly conceived medieval or Japanese animal studies, the beauty of the images will survive their maturing sense of taste. Bright, flat ducks, drawn in prosaic 'child-like' shapes, do not achieve the simplicity they seek, but only provoke boredom or embarrassment in a growing person.

Guest Places

That 'little room', the downstairs loo, the guest's lavatory, call it what you will, creates something of a decorative dilemma. Should it be dismissed in plain, brisk colours as a room to vacate as soon as possible? Why not give it a pretty ornament that belies its necessary purpose?

There is no good reason to withhold a functional wall – white-tiled, perhaps – but there, that splash back over the hand basin, can that not become a focus of visual pleasure? I have already suggested a gorgeous Iznik panel to ornament this area, but this is also the opportunity to set a collection of Victorian or Edwardian tiles into an ornamental pattern. These precious relics will not be exposed to hard or frequent use, or bathroom steam in the guest's lavatory – although, of course, tiles being so hardy are designed to survive extensive daily wear – but also, this area will display them as a special ornament. Incorporated in the family bathroom they might lose their impact or, worse still, look incongruous amongst modern fittings.

Below Monochrome tiled walls and floors do not mean that a practical and visually dull, decoration is achieved. Modern ceramics offer a rich, gleaming range of tones within one colour. *Exim Group.*

The lavatory, on the other hand, is a room which, like the very small kitchen, can carry a bold ornament because there is nothing else to distract the eye, and it does not have the space for objects to accumulate and demand attention.

More and more homes have a separate shower, designed for convenience and ideal for guests. This room, too, can carry an extravagent tile ornament. A large papyrus design, an Art Deco motif frothing across the floor to wall tiling, or a grand geometric abstract, make a positive statement.

Underfoot

Cleanliness is essential in the bathroom and tiling material, so easy to wash down, is the standard wall covering and should cover the floors as well.

Many bathroom floor tiles tend to be laid in simple rectangular rows and are bland in colour – beige or brown. This is to waste an opportunity because the floor, too, can be ornamental. There are tiles with a rustic appearance in muted colours; the tile grid can be laid in diagonals, or keywork patterns; small diamond shapes, or squares, can be laid in contrasting colours. Any decisions should not, of course, conflict with the other tile ornament in the room, but this need not make your floor dull or subdued.

Total Design

This is definitely an area that demands coherent and careful designing. Yes, the bathroom is there simply to keep the body clean, and why all this fuss? The answer to this brisk dismissal of a co-ordinated bathroom design, can be found in the Bauhaus philosophy. It is precisely because this room is purely fuctional that it demands proper, efficient planning and pleasing ornament to make it look and work well.

Below A sophisticated, monochrome-tiled bathroom. *Ganz (Barbee Ceramics).*

CHAPTER 6

Above The range of shape and form within the terracotta tile family is very wide. Neat, rectangular blocks make a 'brick' floor for an outdoor patio. *Ruabon Tiles*.

Far right Indoors, an irregular surface and edging give an 'antique' flooring in a hallway. *Fired Earth*.

Tiles are a wonderful architectural accessory. They make bathrooms and kitchens both hygienic and ornamental, and their use definitely adds to the aesthetic quality of these rooms. Imagine how much duller our cooking and cleaning lives would be without colourful ornamental tiles. But their use need not be restricted to these useful interiors. Take tiles outdoors.

It is worth remembering the sincere social concern of William Morris and William De Morgan, those good Victorians who saw ceramic façades in terms of easy building maintenance. This is not to advocate an entire building covered in utility tiles, or to revert back to the complexity of Islamic mosques, sheathed in shining ornament, but a recommendation that other areas, not just kitchens and bathrooms, would benefit from the practical ornamentation which tiling offers.

More and more architects are giving city-dwellers an access to their own little bit of the outdoors. New buildings incorporate balconies, patios and roof-tops, and cunning inhabitants of older blocks contrive these spaces for themselves. Like a species of nest-makers, city folk use a little balcony area and cover it in geraniums and creepers, with a comfortable chair propped in a corner. Neglected roof areas on the downstairs extension suddenly are transformed into a roof-top patio – more geraniums and creepers proclaim a chance at outdoor living.

Dingy backyard spaces, which once housed coal and rubbish, and perhaps had bicycles or old fridges shoved into them, have become dinky little patios, gay with tubs and a spindly, wrought iron garden table.

All this is splendid, but in a northern climate of inclement weather and cold winters, these little outdoor spaces can begin to look harsh, bare and

Right A floor of quarry slates gives a warm, earthy tone to a dining room. *Fired Earth.*

neglected. Another consideration for many of these small, city fresh-air escapes is that of light – too many of those transformed backyards or roof-top conversions are deprived of direct sunlight, and summer flowers do not thrive in shade.

Quite obviously, then, tiles will serve to transform these spaces. Hard-wearing, immune to weather changes, and ever-colourful, ornamental tiles are a vital architectural accessory in our external world, as much as in our interiors.

Patio or Yard?

The small, grey backyard rectangle has become available as a place to eat 'al fresco', or just sit quietly with the cat and the newspaper. The 'renovation' only required some scrubbing, some whitewash and a few plants to create this extended space. But it still isn't quite as fresh or quite as pleasant as it could be. The concrete floor is depressing and dusty looking. It is dull, and no amount of scrubbing down produces a gleam or shine. Lay a terracotta floor.

Use an unglazed quarry tile, but make sure that it is frost-proof. The warm rustic colours of earth will increase the illusion of country life, and the old grey dinginess of concrete will be permanently banished. Or use those Portuguese tiles that come in a variety of shades. (Refer back to the information on kitchen flooring.) The ivy green of these tiles will echo the plants and give a sense of murmuring colour, even in a patio that is permanently shaded.

Another problem encountered with this kind of patio conversion is the rough walling which may surround it, parts of it covered in plumbing and gas pipes. The white-wash which was slapped on in the optimistic hope that it would spruce up the patio has browned and muddied, or, if there is no surrounding wall but a neglected arch or stair wall above your basement area, the same problem will occur.

Below A comfortable and relaxed living room is given a floor of tiles, laid in a geometric pattern, that does not require the ornament of rugs. *Fired Earth.*

Decorative tiles would solve these twin problems of a clean look and a need for colour.

Design a panel to fit into that overhead wall; choose some of the brilliantly coloured Portuguese tiles, with curly red roosters, narrow vases of tumbling flowers, streamlined birds swooping. The Portuguese tend towards a dense decorative effect – the chief image of the rooster will be surrounded by numerous little motifs, scrolls, stars – and their colours are often of a primary brightness. A panel of

eight or ten of these in a dense, foliate border, will give the patio a lively, vital focus, and the colours will compensate for the lack of blossoms in your shady nook.

The surrounding wall may carry one ornamental device in the same way, but, more likely, it needs a more functional use of tiles. Place a monochrome diaper as high as you can; but fit panel designs, or individual tiles into that. A bold, floral border, or an ornament symbolizing the sun – huge circles – will slice the patio space, and add a welcome division of spatial effect.

Bigger Fry

The established social gathering round the barbeque meal has persuaded many home-owners to build a patio with barbeque area into their gardens. The barbeque pit is often – too often – built of plain brick, but why not use tiles? Design a chic, functional cook-out patio. Build in a work surface round the barbeque pit and ornament it with tiles of a robust character.

Mexican ornament is less sophisticated, but equally decorative. Colours are tropical and warm; the floral and bird designs move happily over the surface, and are a perfect antidote to grey days. The relief of going up to the roof terrace on a blustery autumn day , when old stalks swing about and dead leaves billow, the relief then of seeing beautifully decorated, colourful ornament. The tiles banish that lost, desolate air of the garden-in-the-sky out of season.

Hot House

Exasperation with inclement weather: the longing to live with a sense of space is all too frequently frustrated by rain and wind and cold. All help to persuade many home-owners to enclose that patio area into a conservatory. It is a very intelligent and reasonably inexpensive way of creating another room where the children can play, household sewing can be done, and family teas can be enjoyed.

As with roof terraces, a light-coloured floor enhances the airiness of the glass conservatory. Blend it with your furnishing fabrics and remember how very pleasing the lovely shapes of household plants look, set against a honey or cream flooring. The major ornament in most conservatories comes from these household plants; pots and jars of greenery spread a welcome foliage in the protected atmosphere, and hanging baskets cut the space with tendrils and blossoms.

But this conservatory room is given hard wear – little boys glue their models, tea is spilt, pictures are coloured in or painted. Tables and work surfaces welcome tiles under these living conditions.

This page The traditional browns and golds of terracotta are no longer a conservative design decision. The variety of geometric designs, such as the chevron, or a mix of square and diamond shapes, adds a radical touch to the traditional. Abundant natural light in patios and conservatories blends well with the strong, bright colours of modern technology. *Paris Ceramics; Castelnau Tiles.*

The ingenuity of geometric patterns can be seen on Victorian and Edwardian tiled pathways and entrances. The earliest designers used geometry to create the first repetitive forms, and the tile designers of these paths could draw upon design sources as old as Egypt.

Arrivals and Departures

The Victorians had a very pleasing habit of decorating the entrance steps and the hallway with tiling, and they would carry the tiles up the walls round the front door. They used a lozenge pattern, or diagonal stripes, or a mosaic geometry of practical black and white on the stairs and entrance, but the wall tiles were truly 'art' tiles, offering a visual feast to any arrival at the front door.

Delightful sketches of herbal plants, interspersed with deep green tiles stamped in relief that marked and contrasted the colour and intent of the herb pictures, gave a fresh 'naturalist' welcome. Bird motifs were also favoured; or a copy of Morris' floral work – a flower spread right to the edges of the tile, making an emphatic, rich and proud ornament. A very modern home could present an abstract design of colours and shape to warm and interest the visitor. There are modern replicas of Roman mosaics which form a suitable panel effect on the sides of a door, but Roman gladiators or chariot riders at the entrance of your own home might seem to make rather an odd statement. But here, at last, at the doorway, is the place to make a written statement and use script as ornament. That may entertain your visitors!

That 'lean-to' look of the back porch which was built onto many a Victorian home, can be given some sense of value and permanency through the use of tiles. Not ornamental tiles, perhaps – it is a space that might look incongruous with that kind of visual interest – but brisk efficiency and cleanliness is called for on this back entrance, a place to put boots, and that dog's dish, and the house-plant watering can.

Lozenge patterns, kinetic effects, the ornate interlinking of shapes and angles, duotone or multitone, these pathways are a delightful garden decoration. A tiled doorstep is further enhanced by a wall panel of Art Nouveau floral art tiles.

William Morris and William De Morgan recommended that London homes be sheathed in tiles. This, they pointed out, would allow easy maintenance and resist pollution. The idea was not followed through, but the nineteenth century tile designers modified it to a solution for making tough, yet ornamental pathways and porch entrances. The pathways illustrated here prove the enduring beauty and hardiness of tile decoration. Generations after they were laid they continue to ornament London gardens.

DOULTON & CO., HIGH STREET, LAMBETH, S.E.

DOULTON'S
TERRA COTTA MANTEL PIECES,

In Red or Buff Terra Cotta, with Doulton Ware, Faience, and Mosaic Decorations.

PRICE 20 to 30 GUINEAS, according to design.

Pattern A.G.

Persons requiring a thoroughly artistic and highly decorated stove, will find this arrangement admirably suited to their purpose. The materials are as follows:—Fender Kerb, Side Jambs, Trusses and Mantelshelf are all in Terra Cotta, Fireplace Cheeks and Plinths are of glazed and hand-painted Fire-clay Slabs; the Side Columns, Lower Frieze (of Mosaic) and tiles between the trusses are of Doulton Ware. The Panels above Mantelshelf are in Faience hand-painted Tiles.

Art Pottery of all descriptions, Doulton Ware, Lambeth Faience Hand Painted Tiles, in Enamel or Underglaze, Terra Cotta Vases, Statuettes, &c., for Architecture and Horticulture; Radiating Tile Stoves; Lavatories, Baths, and all descriptions of Sanitary Appliances.

By the Fireside

For centuries fire was of supreme importance in the homes of Northern Europe. In the long winters, before central heating, families never strayed far from their source of warmth – the fireplace. Its importance was not lost on architects and designers, who created wonderful fittings and ornament to enhance the beauty of the functional shape of the fireplace. The Adam brothers in Georgian England were famous for their neo-classical architecture and especially for their surrounds to fireplaces.

But, for lively and colourful ornament surrounding the fireplace the Victorians were the most daring. Realizing the heat-retaining qualities of the tile, they decorated their fireplaces with lavish ornamental ceramics. In their creative hands that dark, sooty space, built into every drawing room and most bedrooms, became a colourful aesthetic statement.

Because the Victorians were so eclectic in their tastes, there is no particular fashion, nor is there any style inhibition in their choice of ornament. Some fireplaces carried wide, tiled panels on either side, decorated with sprays of sprightly, naive flowers, which were painted in light, clear colours. Others were designed in medieval mood, using muted tones with geometric forms complementing the angularity of the fireplace surround. Medieval 'beasties' were occasionally interspersed with this geometry, in imitation of medieval floor designs. A very popular ornament was that which alternated monochrome tiles with decorated tiles. The decoration would consist of flowers or birds, each ornamented tile depicting a different species. This ornament created a richly-chequered and very lively effect.

The Victorian refusal to be restricted to a particular style of ornament is fully demonstrated in the work of William De Morgan. He drew

Below This room repeats the decorative clutter so typical of the last century, and uses a distinctive floral tile ornament bordered in black to enhance the fireplace.
H. & R. Johnson.

inspiration from the Spanish Moors in his brilliantly coloured, curving designs, and from the Turks in his floral ornament. But he also created truly original animal and flower forms. De Morgan made tiles well-suited to side panels of fireplaces, as well as enormous, intricate diapers which covered the wall into which the fireplace was set. Because De Morgan's tile designs were derived from diverse and exotic cultural sources, their popularity has not waned. Manufacturers today produce tiles with similarly eclectic designs, realizing that they have a timeless appeal.

Many designers were extravagant in their use of tiling. Louis Comfort Tiffany created a fireplace in Mr W. S. Kimball's library in Rochester, New York. He covered the entire chimney piece in an intricate mix of monochrome and geometric ornament using zig-zags and the Greek *key*. For Mark Twain's home, he used aquamarine and gold ceramic tiles to brighten the fireplace. Although the Victorian ceramicists used rich and diverse ornament, they all agreed in making the fireplace the visual point of a room. With the introduction of central heating, this focal point was lost and these beautiful fireplaces were often blocked up or demolished.

But now, there is a contemporary longing for the visual pleasure of a fire and the ornament of a fireplace. Technology has brought the realistic flicker and glow of a fire back into our homes, without the back-breaking labour of coal-carrying and soot-cleaning associated with the old fire systems. Many home owners are installing or refurbishing fireplaces, and those beautiful Victorian tiles are enjoying a revival as ornament round these fireplaces. Eager home decorators have taken to searching the junk shops and antique markets for authentic Victorian art tiles, and modern manufacturers also supply excellent copies.

Right An Art Nouveau tiled panel insert for a fireplace. Flowing lines and curves make up a stylized floral design. *The Tile Collection.*

Below Ornate late Victorian tile inserts are shown to great effect in this cast iron, black-leaded fireplace. *Ideal Fireplaces.*

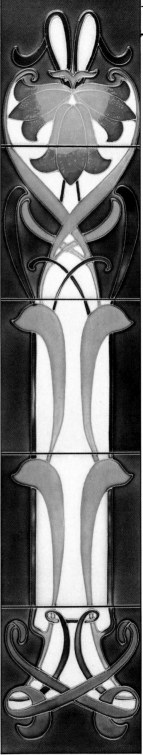

Left Floral 'picture' tiles finely painted in bright, clear colours, were a popular Victorian decoration to off-set a fireplace.

Below Human figures on the 'picture' tile panels of fireplaces are less common, and this Victorian example makes a striking and effective feature on the fireplace.

Left Three samples of Victorian floral 'picture' tile panels for decorating fire-places. *The Tile Collection*.

Below The nineteenth century tile industry employed thousands of craftsmen to satisfy an enormous consumer demand. Ornament was not inhibited by a particular style. *Phillips Fine Art Auctioneers.*

Collecting Art Tiles

The enormous variety in tile ornament does not make it feasible to provide a quick guide for the new collector to consult as he searches for authentic tiles. It is impossible to catalogue or give clear definitions to such an ancient and widespread art. However, most museums have a ceramics department where tiles of many cultures – Chinese, Moorish, Persian, Turkish, English and Mexican – are on display. Visit museums, because a familiarity with the textures, colour and ornament used by all these cultures will help any collector to spot the 'real thing' as he wanders through the antique stalls.

For Victorian enthusiasts, an excellent research source can be found in manufacturers' catalogues, factory pattern books and artists' folios. There are numerous archives where these are available to the public. The famous Wedgwood Museum at Barlaston, England, has an enormous selection in the archives, as has the pottery firm of Spode, who also own the catalogues of Copeland. Stoke-on-Trent, the traditional home of pottery, is worth visiting. Here, the City Reference Library and the Royal Doulton tableware firm both have extensive collections of catalogues and pattern books. These, and the Victoria and Albert Museum in London, are the most famous sources, but enquiries at most museums will lead the collector to fascinating archive material.

The avid collector will also search out antique dealers who specialize in tiles, and learn from the expert. Sadly, as with many other artefacts, art tiles have become valuable on the market, and are reaching prices which many enthusiasts cannot afford. Thirteenth century Islamic tiles can sell for £3,000, and English medieval work is priced at about £350 per tile. A single tile from William De Morgan sells at £400, but, take heart, there are still lovely Victorian and Art Nouveau tiles to be found for £10 or so. Just comb the flea markets!

CHAPTER 7

Any surface that is flat and sound can be easily tiled (for example, plain plaster and plasterboard walls, blockboard, chipboard, plywood and laminated surfaces). Papered or painted walls should be stripped down before tiling them, and where gloss paint has previously been applied, the paint should be checked to ensure a sound surface; concrete surfaces are not ideal for tiling and should only be attempted if in excellent condition. New concrete should be left for at least a month before laying tiles. Hardboard panelled walls should not be tiled with heavy ceramic tiles as the walls will probably not be strong enough to support them, and will eventually sag. When tiling around heat-exposed areas like fireplaces and solid fuel cookers, special thick heat-resistant tiles, made without spacer lugs, should be used in order to resist cracking.

Estimating for tiles

When estimating the amount of tiles you will need to cover an area, measure that area and make allowances for breakages and waste, and cut tiles. Divide the measure of the area to be tiled by the area of one tile, or you can mark off a long batten into tile widths, then hold it vertically and horizontally against the surface to be covered, and multiply the totals together.

Far left A geometric abstract in gleaming contemporary tiles makes a perfect decoration in the modern home. *Ceramiche Cisa.*

Carefully measure the area you want to tile along the length and breadth and work out how many tiles you need by referring to the chart below

Area to be covered										
sq metres	0.6	1.2	1.8	2.4	3.0	3.6	4.2	4.8	5.4	6.0
(sq yds)	(0.7)	(1.4)	(2.2)	(2.9)	(3.6)	(4.3)	(5.0)	(5.7)	(6.5)	(7.2)
Number of tiles needed										
$108mm^2$ ($4\frac{1}{2}in^2$)	50	100	150	200	250	300	350	400	450	500
$152mm^2$ ($6in^2$)	25	50	75	100	125	150	175	200	225	250
Amount of adhesive needed										
(litres)	0.5	1.0	1.5	2.0	2.5	3.0	3.5	4.0	4.5	5.0
Amount of grout needed										
(kilos)	0.2	0.3	0.5	0.6	0.8	1.0	1.1	1.3	1.5	1.6

TECHNIQUES

Ceramic Tile Adhesives

Adhesives are available in powder form, to mix with water, or can be bought ready-to-use. Depending on the type of surface, one can use thin bed, thick bed, waterproof, flexible, or heat-resistant adhesives. Thin bed adhesives should be used on smooth, level surfaces and thick beds on rough, uneven surfaces.

A waterproof grout (rather than water-resistant) should be used where tiles are exposed to water. If tiling a kitchen wall, especially around the sink area, use a grout with an added fungicide for hygienic purposes.

Ceramic edge strip or silicone rubber sealant can be used to seal the gap between the bath and the wall. A flexible rubber-base adhesive, which will stick to tiles, porcelain, and enamel surfaces, is supplied with ceramic edge packs.

Tools

Essential for tiling are a spreader for the adhesive, a tile cutter, a tile ripper, sponge, spirit level and plumb line. A carborundum stone is handy for filing down rough edges after cutting. A masonry drill is necessary for making small holes in tiles, and a radius cutter for making larger holes.

For tiling a large area, a notched trowel is most effective. For smaller areas, a plastic or metal spreader is sufficient. The tiles should be cut with a tungsten carbide tipped scriber.

To cut tiles into shape, pliers or pincers can be used, though special tile rippers are available. Finally, you will need a sponge to apply the grout between the tile joints.

There are many types of adhesive available and it is therefore important to get the right one for the job.	
Ready mixed general purpose adhesive	Suitable for a wide variety of internal surfaces including plaster, paint, concrete, rendering, wood, plywood and old tiles. Not intended for wet service areas where water might penetrate to the adhesive.
Waterproof ceramic tile adhesive	Suitable for 'wet' service areas e.g. showers, splash backs and other areas of the kitchen, bathroom and utility room. Suitable surfaces include plaster, concrete, wood, paint, brick, plasterboard and old tiles.
Waterproof fix and grout	Ready-mixed, dual-purpose adhesive that can also be used as grout. Suitable for all areas described above and sets fast so that tiles can be grouted the same day.
Flexible wall tile adhesive	Intended for use on surfaces liable to some movement, such as lightweight partitions of wood or chipboard, bath panels, boxed-in pipes, etc. It is water resistant but not suitable for areas such as showers or where total immersion occurs.
Wallboard adhesive	Suitable for fixing tiles to worktops and gives table-tops a waterproof bond. It remains perfectly elastic to withstand vibration.
Tile mortar	Cement-based mortar suitable for fixing a wide variety of tile types including ceramic, mosaic, terrazzo and quarry to walls or floors. It will withstand total immersion so is perfect for swimming pools and outside locations.

Tools: 1. Notched trowel. 2. Notched spreader. 3. Squeegee. 4. Sponge. 5. Spirit level. 6. Spacers. 7. Pincers. 8. Tiler cutter. 9. Plumb line.

Tiles: 1. Field tile showing spacer lugs. 2. RE tile. 3. REX tile. 4. Edging pieces.

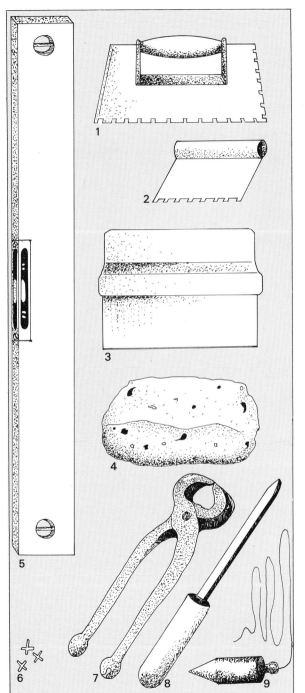

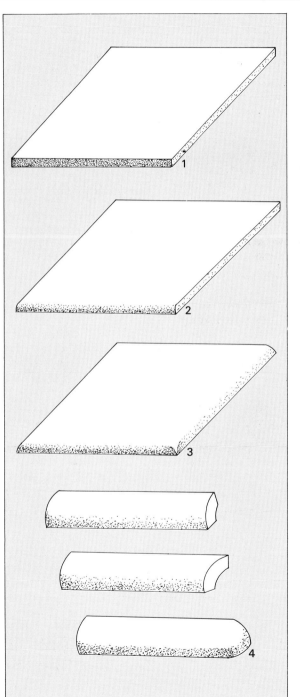

Preparing a Surface for Tiling

Surfaces must be clean, flat, and dry. Any projections should be removed, cracks filled, irregularities levelled and flaking paint removed. Newly plastered surfaces should be left for at least a month before tiling. It is recommended to give painted, stripped or plaster surfaces a coat of stabilizing solution after sanding them down. Loose areas of plaster on old walls should be removed and new plaster applied. Dusty or porous plaster must be sealed with a primer to ensure that the tile adhesive is not absorbed too quickly. In wet areas such as shower cubicles, the best backing is waterproof or exterior grade ply. Don't use chipboard or blockboard as these will expand if they get wet.

Removing Old Ceramic Tiles

Although it is possible to fix new tiles over old ceramic tiles, you cannot decorate over them with paint or wall covering. Hacking off the tiles is very straightforward using a club hammer and bolster chisel. Chop at a shallow angle to avoid gouging the wall when removing the hard adhesive.

Tiling a Wall

Start by making a measuring rod from a long wooden batten. Mark the batten off in divisions of one tile making allowances for the grouting gap between each tile. Attach another batten to the wall, with its upper edge a tile-width above the floor. Use a spirit level to position the batten horizontally. Position the measuring rod on the

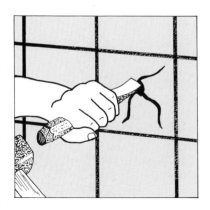

On a completely tiled wall, break the first tile with a cold chisel or by drilling it.

Lever off the tiles by prising the bolster chisel behind one edge and tapping with a hammer.

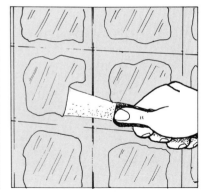

Hack off the adhesive, scraping stubborn areas with the chisel, then fill and smooth. Chop at as shallow an angle as possible to avoid damaging the wall. Prepare the wall as for normal decorating.

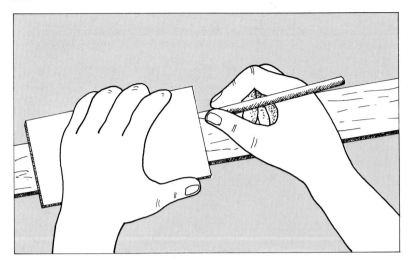

Make a measuring rod from a long wooden batten. Mark the batten off in divisions of one tile plus the grouting gap between each tile. The simplest way to do this is to lay two tiles against the measuring rod with spacers, if you are using them, and then mark across onto the measuring rod.

Attach a batten to the wall with its upper edge one tile width above the floor, using a spirit level to position the batten horizontally. Mark the tile spacing from the measuring rod on the batten. This will act as a support and a guide.

Fit a vertical batten to mark the line of the last row of whole tiles running horizontally. The angle between the battens must be 90°. Check for position with three tiles.

Apply adhesive to the wall over an area of about 1m², using a spreader to form even ridges in the adhesive to the depth of the notches on the spreader.

fixed batten and transfer the tile marks.

At one end of the fixed batten draw a vertical line on the wall, marking the end of the last row of full tiles and fix a batten along it. The angle between the battens must be 90°.

Apply adhesive to the wall over an area of about 1m², using a spreader to form even ridges in the adhesive to the depth of the notches on the spreader. Lay the first tile in the corner where the horizontal and vertical battens meet and press firmly into the adhesive, without sliding it. Lay the next tile on the horizontal batten, touching the spacer lugs of the first tile. Continue working along the horizontal, then lay rows above the first, working in the same way.

Before spreading another area of adhesive, make sure that the tiles are stuck firmly to the adhesive and check the level of the tiles with a spirit level. Continue this process until the main area has been tiled. Let these tiles set for several hours before removing the battens and tiling the ends of the rows where the cut tiles are to be fitted.

When tiling around frames, baths, sinks, basins, and other fittings, you will probably have to fit cut tiles. Tile alongside the fitting first, leaving the area around it until last. Fix a batten at the nearest line of adjacent full tiles above or next to the fitting, and tile above the batten. When the adhesive has set, remove the batten and cut tiles accordingly to fill the remaining space.

When fitting the edges start measuring and cutting along the bottom row and work up the sides

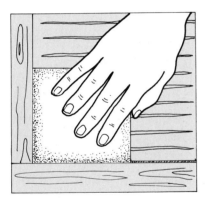

Position the first tile firmly on the adhesive with a slight twisting action, and against the temporary battens.

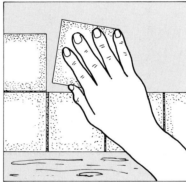

Most types of wall tiles now have spacer lugs on the edges which enable them to be spaced accurately but, if the ones you are using do not, it is possible to buy spacers from a hardware shop. These ensure an even gap around all sides. Tiles should never be placed hard up against each other or hard into the corners of the walls.

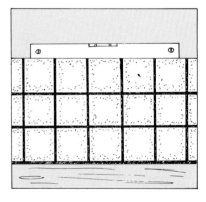

Continue laying the tiles in horizontal rows until the area covered with adhesive is full. Before spreading another area of adhesive make sure that the tiles are firmly stuck and check the level with a spirit level.

afterwards. Once all the tiles have been fitted, leave the adhesive to set for a day and prepare for grouting. You will need two sponges and a thin flat wooden stick with a rounded end. Wipe the grout over the surface of the tiles, rubbing it into the joints with a damp sponge. Excess grout should be wiped off with a dry sponge as you go. Leave for 20 minutes, then run the wooden stick along each joint, pressing the grout in firmly. After a few hours, wipe off the dried remaining grout. Where an accessory, e.g. a soap dish, is to be fitted, fit a field tile temporarily in the intended position and remove it after completing the main area of tiling. Spread adhesive to a thickness of about 2mm over the back of the accessory and press it into place. Tape it to the tiles surrounding it until the adhesive has set.

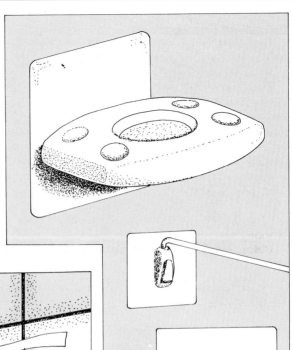

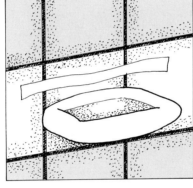

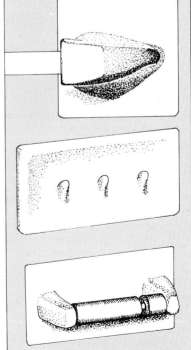

Around window frames, baths, sinks, basins and other fittings leave the cut tiles until last. Fix a batten at the nearest line of adjacent full tiles above or next to the fitting and tile above the batten. When the adhesive has set, remove the batten and cut tiles accordingly.

When fitting an accessory such as a soap dish fit an ordinary or field tile in the intended position and remove it after completing the main area of tiling. Spread adhesive to a thickness of approximately 2mm over the back of the accessory and press it into place. Tape it to the surrounding tiles with masking tape to give it extra support until the adhesive has set.

Cutting and Trimming Tiles

Tiles must be scored with a carbide tipped scorer before the break is made. This prevents the glaze from chipping.

To cut L-shaped tiles to fit around rectangular and square shapes, such as door and window frames and light fittings, hold an uncut tile up against the fitting and mark off with a pen what is to be cut off. Then score over the marking and cut out the un-needed part of the tile with pincers or pliers and,

finally, smooth the cut edges with a filing device.

When cutting a fairly large hole in the middle of a tile you should use a radius cutter. A masonry bit in a hand drill running at low speed is the simplest way to cut small holes in the middle of a tile.

To cut a curved hole at the edge of a tile you will need a round-section blade of carbide fitted into a small hacksaw handle. Mark the shape you want to cut, and saw along it. Smooth the rough edges using a carborundum file.

To prevent the glaze from chipping it must be scored first with a carbide-tipped scorer. Place the tile face up on a flat surface and score the glazed surface along a steel ruler.

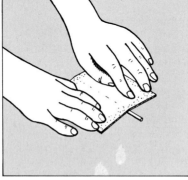

To break the tile place it over a matchstick under each end of the scoreline and press firmly down at each side. The tile should break cleanly.

If you have a lot of tiles to cut it is worth investing in special tile pincers. These have a carbide wheel for scoring and jaws for snapping along the score line.

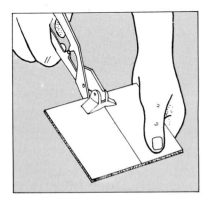

After scoring the tile centre the line in the jaws and squeeze the handles together.

Smooth the cut edge of the tile with a carborundum stone or a special tile file mounted on a piece of wood to remove sharp edges.

Tiling Around Electric Fittings

Be sure that the electricity is switched off at the mains before tiling around electric fittings or switches. With flush-mounted fittings, unscrew the face plate of the fitting and cut the tiles to the edge of the metal box fixed to the wall. Be sure that there is enough room for the face plate and its attached wires to go back freely. Grout the joints behind the face plate thoroughly before screwing it back into place.

Tiling Angles and corners

The general rule is that one should use full tiles at outer angles and corners, and cut tile in inner angles and corners. This rule is also applicable to window and door reveals. At outer angles it is advisable to nail a batten to the return wall and lay one wall of tiles flush with the edge of the wall, and overlap their sides with the adjacent row after removing the batten. For a neat finish lay RE (round-edge) tiles on the return wall to overlap the exposed edges of the adjacent tiles. Cut tiles are best left to inner corners where they will be less obtrusive.

If you are tiling over an old area of tiling which goes only half way up the wall, there will be the problem of a small step. A simple way of levelling the wall is to stick hardboard to the untiled section of the wall, using contact adhesive. Be sure to use waterproof hardboard in a kitchen or bathroom.

To cut L-shaped tiles mark the area to be cut out and score over the marking. Make sure that the scores do not extend beyond the meeting point. Then score the waste section in a criss-cross fashion.

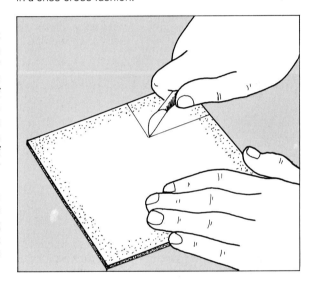

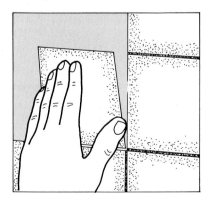

Fix the cut tile so that the spacer lugs are against those of the adjoining and the cut edge goes into the corner where it will be less obtrusive.

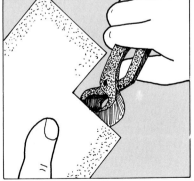

Nibble away the waste piece by piece using a pair of pliers or pincers, being careful not to bite too much.

Use the flat jaw of the pincers to nibble the tile up to the edge of the score.

Measure and cut the hardboard sheets to fit the area and fix the pieces one section at a time. Sand down the glossy side of the hardboard and spread the adhesive with a serrated spreader. Concentrate on getting even coverage along the edges and corners when applying the adhesive. Smooth the sheet into position on the wall while the adhesive is still wet, thus transferring the glue to the wall and indicating the area on the wall that must be coated with adhesive. Spread the adhesive on the wall, and when both surfaces are touch-dry, press the hardboard firmly into place on the wall. Allow the adhesive to dry completely before fixing the tiles.

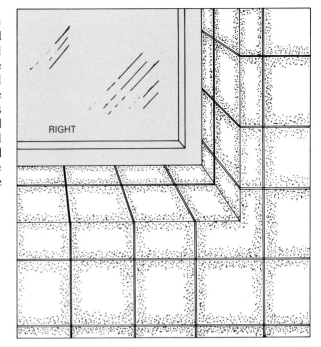

Plan the tiling so that it is arranged symmetrically around doors and windows, with the odd spaces taken up with cut tiles at the ends of walls, and not in the middle where it would be particularly noticeable. Position cut tiles on window ledges and recesses at the back and not the front.

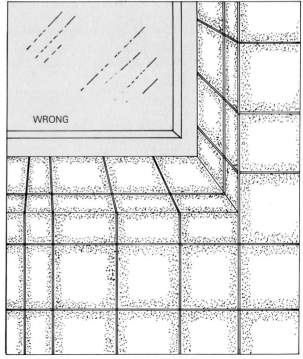

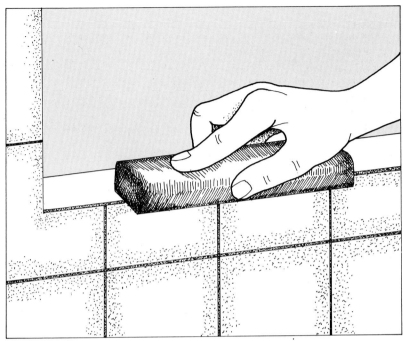

At outer corners lay one row of tiles flush with the edge of the wall and use a carborundum stone to level off adjoining edges of cut tiles.

Fit RE (round-edged) tiles to overlap the ends of adjacent row.

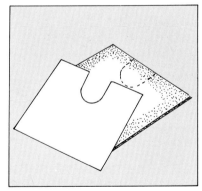

To cut a ceramic tile to fit round curved objects such as pipes can be done by making straight cuts and filling with grout, but it does not look very neat. The better alternative is to make a paper template of the cut out and transfer it to the glazed surface of the tile.

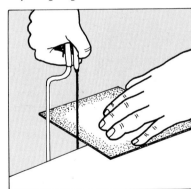

Remove the waste using a rod saw. This is simply a round-section blade of carbide which is fitted into a small hacksaw handle. Smooth down the edges with a carborundum file.

Some people are sensitive to cement powder and it is therefore advisable to wear rubber gloves when grouting and not to keep running your fingers along the joints to smooth the grout.

Tile grout	White waterproof grout for use with waterproof tile adhesives. It is supplied in powder form, for mixing with water.
Ready-mixed coloured grouts	As above but with the option of ready-mixed colour in a variety of shades to tone or contrast with your tiles.
Epoxy worktop grout	Completely non-porous and waterproof and therefore ideal for kitchen worktops as it cannot hold dirt or germs.
Floor tile grout	Grey waterproof grout, suited for use with tile mortar for internal and external use.

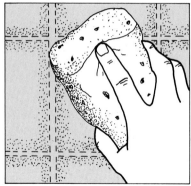

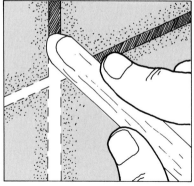

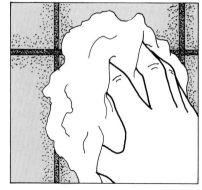

Give the tiling at least 24 hours to dry, and then fill the gaps between the tiles with an appropriate grout. Make up the grout following the manufacturer's instructions or buy ready-mixed and apply it with a sponge or the straight edge of a spreader, making sure all the joints are properly filled.

Pack the grout firmly into the joints and smooth off using a small rounded stick.

Remove any grouting material left on the tiles with a damp cloth, rinsing frequently in clean water. Polish the tiles with a clean, dry cloth after the grout has set.
 A permanently flexible sealant is needed to give adhesion to glazed tiles when sealing joints round baths and showers etc.

Ceramic and quarry tile floors are very hardwearing, easy to clean and waterproof. They are also, however, noisy, hard on the feet and cold to walk on. Before tiling a floor, the surface has to be sound, firm and level. Uneven concrete, loose floorboards, damp old linoleum or pitted asphalt are typical floor problems that must be dealt with before laying the tiles.

When buying ceramic tiles, check whether they are suitable for flooring, as wall tiles are too brittle for floors.

Determine a laying plan

Designs in floor tiles should start from the centre of the room for symmetry, although borders at the walls must be taken into account as well. Borders should be as equal and as wide as possible, so as to avoid having to cut narrow or awkward pieces. If this means moving the starting point in the middle, then do so.

Individual tiles should be symmetrical to the main doorway of the room. This could be rather difficult in an awkwardly shaped room. First, you must determine the centre of the room. If the room is square or rectangular, find the centre of two opposite walls and stretch a chalked stringline between these points. Snap the line to chalk the floor. Repeat this for the other two walls. Where the lines cross is the centre of the room.

A Room With Awkward Angles

In a room with awkward angles, use the method

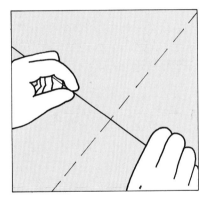

To plan the layout, find the middle point of two facing walls and fix a nail at each of these points about 25mm up from the floor. Then rub a length of string thoroughly with chalk and tie it tightly between the nails. Lift the string and let it snap down quickly to leave a chalk line across the floor. Remove the string and repeat the operation running another length at right angles to the first. Where the chalk lines cross is the centre point of the room.

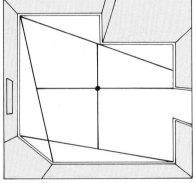

To determine the centre point of an awkwardly shaped room, measure between the opposite walls avoiding the obstructions. Connect the mid points of the lines and this will give the centre of the room.

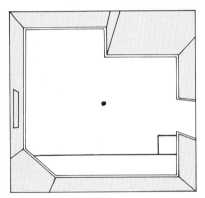

To enable tiles to be laid square to the door stretch a string at right angles over to the facing wall.

shown in the diagram below to find the centre point of the room. Use tiles in a 'dry-laying' sequence or a gauge batten marked off in tile increments (plus joints where relevant) to plot the rows on the floor, altering the starting point to avoid bad cuts and narrow corners.

Preparing Floors for Tiling

If tiling over wooden floors, nail or screw down any loose boards and remove insecure nails and screws. Wooden floors should be covered with plywood or hardboard. Suspended wooden floors at ground level must always remain well ventilated if damp and rot are to be avoided. With concrete floors the most common problem is dampness. If the floor is damp it must be treated with waterproofing compound.

Pitting and general unevenness can be repaired by using a self-levelling compound. Pour this over the floor area, following the manufacturer's instructions closely. To fill larger holes, make up a mortar mix. Add just enough water to make the mix malleable, and some plasticizer to minimize shrinkage during drying.

Laying Ceramic Floor Tiles

Work out your laying plan for the tiling, then, because ceramic floor tiles are best laid from one corner of the room, nail temporary right-angled battens at the perimeter of the area of whole tiles you are working in. Work towards the door, as you shouldn't walk on the tiles for 24 hours.

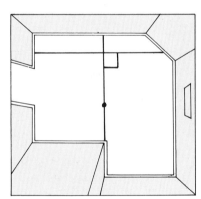

Stretch a second string at right angles to the first string across the centre point of the room.

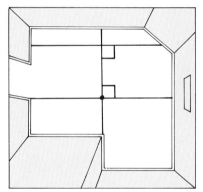

A third string stretched across the room parallel to the first completes the laying guide. When the laying guide is determined chalk the string lines and snap them onto the floor to mark it as already described.

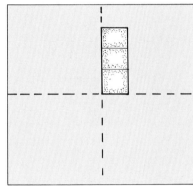

Dry lay a row of tiles and check that the tiles fitted against the walls do not have to be cut too narrowly; note how tiles will fit into awkward angles.

A special flooring adhesive is needed for laying the floor tiles down. Most varieties are sold ready-mixed. For areas susceptible to water, choose a waterproof type. A cement-based adhesive is suitable for concrete floors, but a flexible, cement/rubber type must be used on timber floors.

Once the first chalked area is completed, remove the battens, place them in the adjoining corner of the room, and repeat the procedure.

Once the field tiles can be walked on, fit the border tiles. Finally, the gaps between each tile must be grouted. To grout floor tiles, follow the same procedure as with wall tiles. Check with the grouting chart shown on page 140. A tile cutter or jig is best for cutting them to size.

Tile mortar: A cement-based adhesive for fixing a wide variety of tile-types both including quarry tiles inside and out which will withstand any amount of water immersion.

Ready-mixed waterproof fix and grout: A buff coloured dual purpose adhesive and grout for fixing ceramic floor tiles to concrete, old tiles, vinyl tiles and wooden floors.

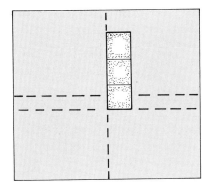

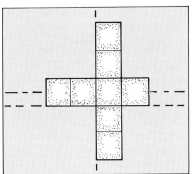

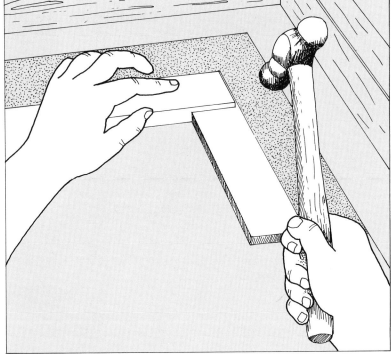

Adjust the layout to a new centre point if it improves the layout and avoids narrow margins.

Fit temporary right-angled guide battens at the perimeter of the 'field' of whole tiles. Ceramic tiles are laid from one corner of the room.

Remember to work towards the door as the tiles should not be walked on for 24 hours.

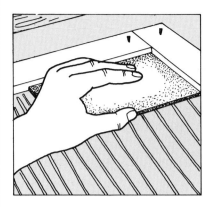

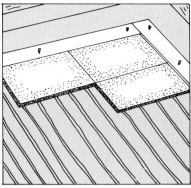

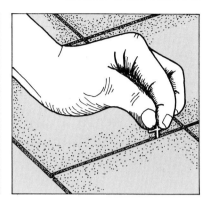

Spread the adhesive onto the floor in an area of about 1 square metre, using a notched spreader.
Start at the corner formed by the guide battens, pressing the tile firmly into position with a slight twisting action to bed the tile properly.

Press the second and third tiles onto the floor butted against the first tile's exposed edge. Make sure that the whole of the back of each tile is in contact with the adhesive and that no hollows are left underneath. Spread extra adhesive on the back of the tile if necessary, because it is very important to support each tile with adhesive across its entire area, to avoid the possibility of the tiles cracking.

If the tiles don't have built in spacers fit spacing pegs between each tile to ensure an even gap around all sides. These can be obtained from your tile supplier or, alternatively, use pieces of cardboard, but ensure that these are a uniform thickness of approximately 1mm (1/16in).

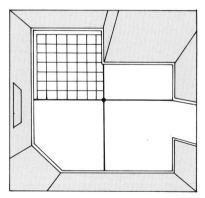

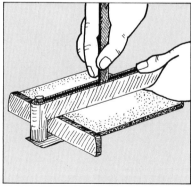

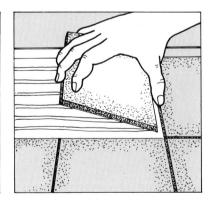

Work diagonally from the corner until the first bay formed by the chalk lines is filled. Before the adhesive sets, clean off any surplus and clean up the tile joints in readiness for grouting. Repeat the procedure until all the bays are completed. When the floor can be walked on (after about 24 hours) fit the border tiles.

Ceramic floor tiles are much thicker and stronger than wall tiles but it is possible to cut them with a special tile cutting tool. However, some retailers hire out easy-to-use tile cutters. For grouting, refer to the section on wall tiles.

The cut edge of the tile should be set against the wall, making a perfect fit after the spacing pegs have been fitted.

When laying a quarry tile floor the tiles are laid on a screed of dryish mortar and extra care should be taken to make sure that the mortar bedding is smooth and level. It is recommended that battens be fixed to the floor at exact distances apart, corresponding to about six tiles plus 3mm joins. The battens can then be levelled and provide a form work for the mortar. (In the same way a tamping board is used when laying a concrete pathway).

Quarry tiles should be fixed with a mix of one part cement to three parts sand to which a PVA agent has been added.

Make a tamping board with a notch at either end Fill the space with the mortar, then spread the mortar out by moving the board backwards and forwards. Then, while the mortar is still wet, lay the quarry tiles flush with the top of the battens and align them with consistent spaces in between.

With the first bay of quarry tiles fitted, remove the inside dividing batten and move it over to form a second bay, levelling and aligning as before. Continue this pattern until the entire area of whole tiles is in position.

It is better to leave the floor overnight before removing the perimeter battens and cutting and fitting the border tiles. Grouting can then follow. Remove the battens, and use a rubber squeegee to grout the joints with cement.

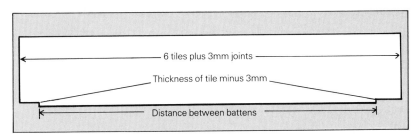

6 tiles plus 3mm joints

Thickness of tile minus 3mm

Distance between battens

Make a tamping board, with a notch at either end which is the thickness of a tile minus 3mm.

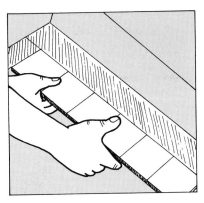

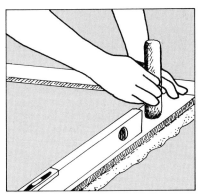

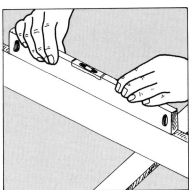

The floor should be divided up into bays, six tiles wide. Nail perimeter battens to the floor, then use a tiling gauge to plot positions of the bay battens.

Set the bay-dividing battens in mortar and level them along their length by tapping gently.

Check across the bay battens with a spirit level, packing up or tapping down as necessary. The battens will provide a formwork for the mortar in the same way as when laying a concrete path.

TECHNIQUES

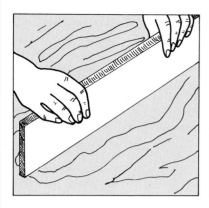

Fill the space between the battens with mortar and then level it to one tile thickness below the battens by moving the tamping board backwards and forwards.

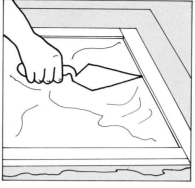

Trowel a thin mixture of cement and water over the mortar base to improve tile adhesion.

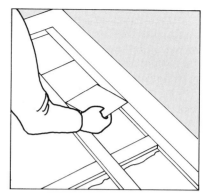

Place the first row of tiles against the battens and position them with the aid of the tiling gauge, inserting spacer pegs to ensure even spacing between the tiles.

Lay the first 16 or so tiles. Tap them gently with a wooden block until they are level with the batten and check with a spirit level.
Straighten the tiles by running the trowel along the joints.

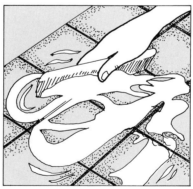

Remove the third batten and refix to form another bay. Repeat the process as before, levelling and aligning the bay with the first bay, until the floor is finished. Fill the gaps around the edge of the floor with cut tiles and when the tiles are set (after 24 hours), grout as previously described.

Spread sawdust and work it over the tiles with a cloth to clean them and absorb any bits of cement, rubbing first diagonally and then across the joints. Sweep up the remainder of sawdust and rub over the tiles with a clean cloth. For outside use boiled linseed oil should be rubbed into the tiles. For inside use finish with a proprietary tile polish.

Mosaic floors are becoming increasingly popular again and are easy and quick to lay if you buy the mosaic tiles sold in paper-backed sheet form. Individual mosaic tiles can either be square or rectangular.

The floor should be marked up and battened in exactly the way described earlier for floor tiles. Apply the adhesive to the floor surface with a notched trowel/spatula. It is best to start in a corner that has been laid out with battens.

Then, using a trowel, apply grout to the back of a sheet of mosaic, in other words, to the side that will lie face down on the floor and be hidden from view. The paper-backed side must lie facing upwards.

Sufficient grout must be used for you to be able to press it into the gaps between individual mosaic tiles. This is best done using a rubber squeegee.

After doing this, you must lay the sheet (paper-backing side up, grout side down) quickly onto the prepared adhesive surface. it is important to do this quickly so as to avoid letting the water in the grout saturate the paper-backing and loosen it. Once a sheet has been positioned, other sheets should be spaced around it and a space equal to the distance between each mosaic tile should be left between separate sheets. A small piece of folded cardboard or wood placed between sheets can help you to maintain equal spacing between sheets. It is best to lay no more than one square metre of sheets at a time. To ensure that the individual tiles are evenly and well embedded in the adhesive, use a block of wood and a hammer, or a home-made wooden tool, to tamp the sheets of mosaic down hard. Excess adhesive should be removed from the area surrounding the sheets, before you begin to lay the next square metre of mosaic sheets.

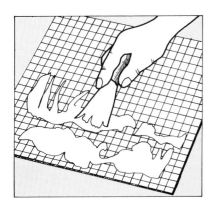

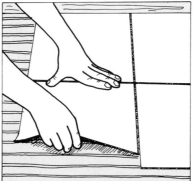

Prepare the floor as previously described and apply the relevant adhesive.
Apply grout to the non-papered side of the mosaic sheet and, using a squeegee, press the grout into all the spaces between the tiles, so that no gaps remain. The paper-backed side will lie facing upwards when the sheet has been laid.

Lay the sheet fairly quickly onto the prepared adhesive surface, so that the paper backing on the top surface does not become too saturated by the water from the grout and does not begin to peel off. The sheets of mosaic should be positioned with a space left between each sheet equal to the space between each mosaic tile. To help do this accurately, a small piece of card or wood, of the correct size, can be placed between sheets and removed before grouting between sheets.

Use a block of wood and a hammer, or a homemade wooden tool (as shown) to tamp the sheets down evenly and firmly, so that the mosaic tiles are properly embedded in the adhesive. It is best to lay no more than one square metre of mosaic sheets at a time. Excess adhesive should be removed from the surrounding area before laying the next section.

Once the main area of the floor is completely covered, you can remove the battens and cut up sheets of mosaic to fit the gaps around the edge of the room. You may have to score individual tiles and use a pair of pincers to break them if complete mosaic tiles do not quite fit the gaps at the edges. (The procedure for laying these smaller sections of mosaic sheet is the same as that described above.)

Leave the adhesive to set for about 24 hours before you walk on the floor. Then soak the papered surface of the floor thoroughly with a sponge and gently peel off the paper.

After removing the paper, you will need to fill in the spaces between the separate sheets of mosaic with grout. A squeegee is best used for this. Once the grout has set and dried you can wipe off any surplus and your mosaic floor is finished!

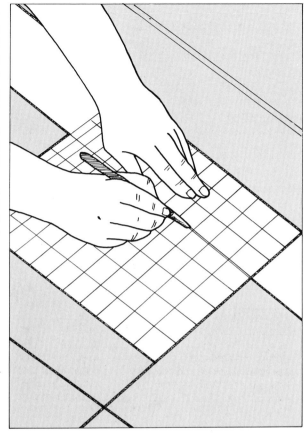

When the main area of floor is tiled, you can fill in the gaps around the edge of the room. Remove the battens and mark the section of the sheet to be cut after placing it upside-down (paper side down) over the untiled area. You may need to cut individual tiles by scoring them and then using pincers.

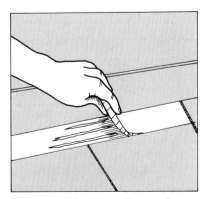

Apply adhesive to the floor surface, grout the small sections of mosaic sheet and lay them following the same method as before.

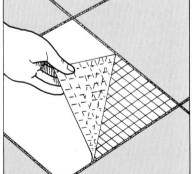

Leave the adhesive to set for 24 hours before walking on the floor. When set, soak the paper surfaces with a sponge and gently peel off the paper to reveal the mosaic floor.

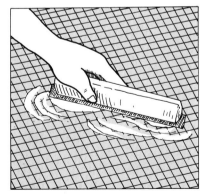

You will finally need to fill the spaces between the sheets with grout. This is done with a squeegee and then left for a few minutes. Afterwards, wipe off the surplus with a cloth.

If a ceramic tile is cracked or completely broken, you can remove it by breaking it up with a hammer and a small chisel. Start at the centre of the tile to avoid damaging surrounding tiles. (If you are dealing with a broken quarry tile, surrounding tiles may not be firmly embedded and you can lift them out.) The underlaying adhesive must be removed carefully with a chisel and the surface evened out. Lay the new tile in position, dry, to make sure that it does not project above floor level. Any tile replaced should be of exactly the same size and thickness as the existing tiles. If only one or two tiles are to be replaced, use a rubber-based adhesive and slot them in. You will need to apply grout to fill the gaps between the old and new tiles. When replacing many tiles, hack up the bedding and relay them in the same way that you would lay a new floor.

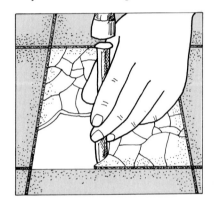

Carefully tap across the top of any cracked tile to craze and crack the whole surface. Working from the centre of the tile chip out fragments with a small cold chisel.

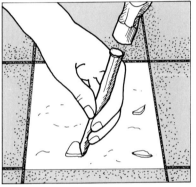

Use the chisel to smooth the underneath surface and remove as much old adhesive or cement as possible. Scrape out the corners and brush away surplus dust.

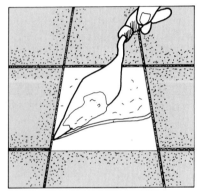

Place the new tile in position to check that it is level and just below the surface of the adjacent tiles. Remove the tile and spread on a thin layer of adhesive.

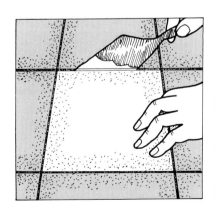

Press the tile into position, straightening the joints with a trowel. Remove any excess adhesive. After 24 hours the tile can be grouted as described previously.

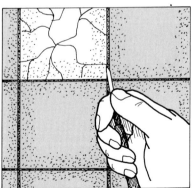

In the case of wall tiles, dig out the grouting cement from all sides with a sharp pointed scraper.

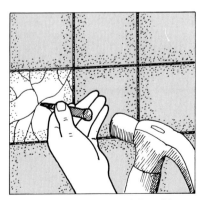

Chip away the damaged tile with a hammer and chisel, removing as much old adhesive as possible; replace the tile as previously described.

UK MANUFACTURERS

A G Tiles
Dividy Road
Bucknall
Stoke-on-Trent
Staffs ST2 0JB
Tel: 0782 313981

Sally Anderson Tiles
Parndon Mill
Harlow
Essex CM20 2HP
Tel: 0279 20982

The Art Tile Company Ltd
Etruria Tile Works
Garner Street
Etruria
Stoke-on-Trent ST4 75B
Tel: 0782 29819

Laura Ashley
183 Sloane Street
London SW1 (and branches)
Tel: 01-235 9728

Badger Tiles
125 Main Road
Long Hanborough
Oxford
Tel: 0993 882280

Candy Tiles Ltd
Heathfield
Newton Abbot
Devon TQ12 6RF
Tel: 0626 832641

Ceramiche Cisa
(UK agent: Edgar Aquilina
Tel: 01-994 0351 for list
of UK stockists.)

Margery Clinton Ceramics
The Pottery
Newton Port
Haddington
East Lothian
Tel: 062 082 3584

Danielle Ltd
148 Walton Street
London SW3 2JJ
Tel: 01-584 4242

Domus Ltd
266 Brompton Road
London SW3
Tel: 01-589 9457

Faenza
Unit 4, Manford Estate
Manor Road
Erith
Kent DA8 2AJ
Tel: 0322 332211

Fired Earth
Middle Aston
Oxfordshire OX5 3PX
Tel: 0869 40724

Eleanor Greeves
12 Newton Grove
Bedford Park
London W4 1LB
Tel: 01-994 6523

H & R Johnson Tiles Ltd
Highgate Tile Works
Tunstall
Stoke-on-Trent
Tel: 0782 85611

Hereford Tiles Ltd
Whitestone
Hereford HR1 3SF
Tel: 0432 850381

Lambeth Tiles
12-14 Pensbury Street
London SW8
Tel: 01-720 4511

Marlborough Ceramic Tiles
Elcot Lane
Marlborough
Wilts
Tel: 0672 52422

Maw & Co Ltd
342 High Street
Tunstall
Stoke-on-Trent
Tel: 0782 817341

Daniel Platt & Sons Ltd
Brownhills Tileries
Tunstall
Stoke-on-Trent
Tel: 0782 86187

Pipe Dreams
2 Hinde Street
London W1M 4RH
Tel: 01-486 1064

Sylvia Robinson
63 The Hundred
Romsey
Hampshire SO51 7NJ
Tel: Romsey 514930

Maria Rosenthal
Kingsgate Workshop
110-116 Kingsgate Road
London NW6 2JS
Tel: 01-328 2051

Dennis Ruabon Ltd
Haford Tileries
Ruabon
Wrexham
Clwyd
Tel: 0978 842283

Rye Tiles
12 Connaught Street
London W2 2AF
Tel: 01-723 7278

Jennifer Scott
Coach Hill House
Burley Street
Ringwood
Hants
Tel: 04253 3361

Skye Ceramics Ltd
238-240 Brompton Road
London SW3 2BB
Tel: 01-584 9818

Sphinx Tiles Ltd
Bath Road
Colthrop Lane
Thatcham
Berkshire
Tel: 0635 65475

Tessera Designs
Wemco
Whippendell Road
Watford
Herts
Tel: 0923 46959

Alghero Tilecraft
Haslemere Crossroads
High Wycombe HB15 7LG
Tel: 0494 711212

Bernard J Arnull & Co
13-14 Queen Street
London W1
Tel: 01-499 3231

Barbee Ceramics Ltd
Merton Works
Church Road
Welling
Kent
Tel: 01-855 9644

A Bell & Co Ltd
Kingsthorpe Road
Kingsthorpe
Northampton NN2 6LT
Tel: 0604 712505

Brausch & Co
The Gate Centre
Great West Road
Brentford
Middlesex TW8 9DD
Tel: 01-847 4455

Bristol Tile Company Ltd
543-554 Fishponds Road
Fishponds
Bristol BS16 3DQ
Tel: 0272 650921

B J Brown (London) Ltd
659 Holloway Road
London N19
Tel: 01-263 7283

Capital Ceramics
Priors House
Beaumont Road
London E13 8RJ
Tel: 01-471 8121

Capitol Tile Supplies Ltd
Eagle Street
Coventry CV1 2RJ
Tel: 0203 58391

Carmona Tiles
40 Curzon Street
London W1
Tel: 01-499 7804

Castelnau Mosaic & Tiles of Barnes Ltd
175 Church Road
Barnes
London SW13
Tel: 01-741 2452

Ceramic Tile Distributors PLC
Ceramic House
72 Hydepark Street
Glasgow G3 8BW
Tel: 041 221 4591

Ceramic Tile Distributors
(Newcastle) Ltd
162 Brinkburn Street
Newcastle-upon-Tyne NE6 2AR
Tel: 091 276 1506

Ceramic Tile Distributors
(Yorks) Ltd
Ceramic House
Hartley Street
off Wakefield Road
Bradford BD4 7NL
Tel: 0274 306308

Ceramica & Il Bagno Ltd
794 Fulham Road
London SW6 5SL
Tel: 01-736 7251

Ceramic World
4 The Green
Winchmore Hill
London N21
Tel: 01-886 1320

Continental Tiles Ltd
8 Haycroft Road
Stevenage
Herts
Tel: 0438 724808

Cornwise Ltd
168 Old Brompton Road
London SW5
Tel: 01-373 6890

Creta Ceramica (Midlands) Ltd
Unit 4, Walton Industrial Estate
Stone
Staffs ST15 0NN
Tel: 0785 815664

Croft Brothers (London) Ltd
7a Coppetts Road
London N10 1NP
Tel: 01-444 0222

Cubic Metre
17-18 Great Sutton Street
London EC1
Tel: 01-253 7557

Elizabeth Eaton
25a Basil Street
London SW3 1BB
Tel: 01-589 0118

Elite Tiles (London) Ltd
Unit S1A, Cricklewood Trading Estate
Claremont Road
London NW2
Tel: 01-452 6358

Elon Tiles UK Ltd
8 Clarendon Cross
Holland Park
London W11
Tel: 01-727 0884

Exim Trading (UK) Ltd
Unit 55a, Milton Trading Estate
Abingdon
Oxon OX14 4AX
Tel: 0235 834192

Flooring Supplies Ltd
Bernard Works
Bernard Road
London N15 4NE
Tel: 01-808 3011

Galaxy Tiles Ltd
Amber Business Centre
Hilltop Road
Riddings
Derbyshire DE55 4BR
Tel: 0773 606060

David Gillespie Associates Ltd
Dippenhall Crossroads
Farnham
Surrey
Tel: 0252 723531

Hannibal Ceramics Ltd
68 Lambs Conduit Street
London WC1
Tel: 01-405 6016

Langley London Ltd
The Tile Centre
161-167 Borough Hill Street
London SE1
Tel: 01-407 4444

Lyfestyle Interiors
104 Allitsen Road
London NW8
Tel: 01-586 3357

Miles of Tiles
Norman Road
Rangemoor Industrial Estate
London N15 4NE
Tel: 01-801 5331

Panceramic Ltd
Eldon Way
Crick
Northants
Tel: 0788 822129

Pandel Tiles (N.I.) Ltd
97 Ravenhill Road
Belfast BT6 8DQ
Tel: 0232 458805

Paris Ceramics
543 Battersea Park Road
London SW11 3BL
Tel: 01-228 5785

V Parkin & Son Tiles Ltd
Barton Park
Barton
N Yorks DL10 6NF

Ramus Tile Co Ltd
Palace Road
London N11 2PX
Tel: 01-881 2345

W Richardson Tiles Ltd
16-19 Sir John Rogersons Quay
Dublin 2
Tel: 0001 772884

Taylor Tiles (South Wales) Ltd
Beaufort Road
Plasmarl Industrial Estate
Morriston
Swansea SA6 8JG
Tel: 0792 797712

The Tile Collection
60 Fortune Green Road
London NW6
Tel: 01-431 0900

Tiles of Newport and London
Dumfries Place Estate
Dumfries Place
Newport
Gwent
Tel: 0633 50383

Tiles, Tiles, Tiles
168 Old Brompton Road
London SW5
Tel: 01-373 6890

Verity Tiles Ltd
7 Jerdan Place
Fulham Broadway
London SW6 1BE
Tel: 01-245 9000

Waxman International Ltd
Grove Mills
Elland
West Yorks
Tel: 0422 71811

World's End Tiles
9 Langton Street
London SW10
Tel: 01-351 0279

ARIZONA
Facings of America
4121 North 27th Street
Phoenix, AZ 85016
602-955-9217

CALIFORNIA
Eurobath & Tiles
Design Center South
23811 Aliso Creek Road Ste. #155
Laguna Niguel
CA 92677
714-643-5033

Southwestern Ceramics
999 Rancheros Dr.
San Marcos
CA 92069
619-741-2033

Southwestern Ceramics
5525 Gaines Street
San Diego
CA 92110
619-298-3511

Tilecraft
Galleria Design Center
101 Henry Adams St #226
San Francisco
CA 94103
415-552-1913

Walker Zanger
8914 Beverly Blvd
Los Angeles
CA 90048
213-278-8664

Walker Zanger
2960 Airway Ave #B-140
Costa Mesa
CA 92626
714-546-3671

Walker Zanger
1832 S. Brand Blvd
Glendale
CA 91204
213-245-6927

COLORADO
Euro Bath
1801 Wynkoop Ste #380
Denver
CO 80202
303-298-8453

CONNECTICUT
Town & Country
PO Box 469
Avon
CT 06001
203-677-6965

Waterworks
11 Newtown Road
Danbury
CT 06810
203-792-9979

Waterworks
226 Post Rd East
West Port
CT 06880

FLORIDA
Sunny McLean & Co
3800 NE Second Ave
Miami
FL 33137
305-573-5943

GEORGIA
Traditions in Tile
A.D.A.C.
351 Peachtree Hills Ave NE #140
Atlanta
GA 30305
404-239-9186

Traditions in Tile
585 Atlanta Street
Roswell
GA 30075
404-998-0155

ILLINOIS
Euro Tec Tiles Inc
Merchandise Mart #1307
Chicago
IL 60654
312-329-0077

KANSAS
Tile Source Inc
6420 W 110th St #104
Overland Park
KS 66211
913-345-8453

MASSACHUSETTS
Tiles, A Refined Selection, Inc
115 Newbury Street
Boston
MA 02116

Tiles, A Refined Selection, Inc
Boston Design Center
One Design Center Place Ste #633
Boston
MA 02210

MICHIGAN
Virginia Tile
Michigan Design Center
1700 Stutz #22
Troy
MI 48084
313-649-4422

Virginia Tile
22201 Telegraph Rd
Southfield
MI 48034
313-353-4250

MINNESOTA
Fantasia Showroom
I.M.S. Design Center
275 Market Street #102
Minneapolis
MN 55405
612-338-5811

NEW JERSEY
Terra Cotta
Princeton Forrestal Village
124 Stanhope Street
Princeton
NJ 08540
609-520-0075

NEW YORK
Carminart
61 N Central Ave
Elmsford
NY 10523
914-592-6330

Shelly Tile
D & D Bldg 8th Floor
979 Third Ave
New York
NY 10022
212-832-2255

NORTH CAROLINA
McCullough Ceramics
5272 Germanton Road
Winston Salem
NC 27105
919-744-0660

OHIO
Hamilton Parker Co
165 W Vine Street
Columbus
OH 43215
614-221-6593

OKLAHOMA
Paschal Tile
10918 E 55th Place
Tulsa
OK 74146
918-622-0017

OREGON
United Tile
3435 SE 17th Street
Portland
OR 97202
503-231-4959

PENNSYLVANIA
Tile Collection
4031 Bigelow Blvd
Pittsburgh
PA 15213
412-621-1051

Tile Shop of Society Hill
621 South Second Street
Philadelphia
PA 19147
215-923-3448

TENNESSEE
Tile Contractors Supply Company
2548 Bransford Ave
Nashville
TN 37204
615-269-9669

TEXAS
French Brown Floors
7007 Greenville Ave
Dallas
TX 75231
214-363-4341

Southwest Tile
1375 E Bitters Rd
San Antonio
TX 78216
512-491-0057

Walker Zanger
11500 South Main #124
Houston
TX 77025
713-664-8811

Walker Zanger
The Interior Resource Center
7026 Old Katy Rd #219
Houston
TX 77024
713-861-7745

UTAH
Florida Tile Ceramic Center
305 West 2880 South
Salt Lake City
UT 84115
801-485-2900

WASHINGTON
United Tile
17400 W Valley Rd
PO Box 58204
Tukwilla Branch
Seattle
WA 98188
206-251-5290

WISCONSIN
Childcrest Distributor
6045 N 55th Street
Milwaukee
WI 53218
414-462-9770

NEW SOUTH WALES
The Olde English Tile Factory,
73-79 Parramatta Road,
Camperdown NSW 2050
(02) 519 4333

Classic Ceramics,
25 Balmain Road,
Leichhardt NSW 2040
(02) 560 6555

Selective Tile Centre,
658 Botany Road,
Alexandria NSW 2015
(02) 669 6255

Graham's Tile Centre,
561 Botany Road,
Waterloo NSW 2017
(02) 699 8888

VICTORIA
Mingarelli Tiles,
11 Nelson Street,
Moorabbin Vic. 3189
(03) 555 9766

Classic Ceramics,
93 Queensbridge Street,
South Melbourne Vic. 3205
(03) 62 6691

Signorino Ceramics,
847 Sydney Road,
Brunswick Vic. 3056
(03) 383 1788

SOUTH AUSTRALIA
Classic Tiles,
41 North Terrace,
Adelaide SA 5000
(08) 212 5466

QUEENSLAND
Classic Ceramics,
84 Annerley Road,
Woolloongabba Qld 4102
(07) 393 1022

WESTERN AUSTRALIA
Crosby Tiles,
46 Hector Street,
Osborne Park WA 6017
(09) 446 6000

TASMANIA
The Tile Centre,
287 Main Road,
Glenorchy Tas., 7010
(002) 72 8874

Arlington Mill Museum
Bibury
Gloucestershire
Tel: 078574 368

The Bowes Museum
Barnard Castle
County Durham DL12 8NP
Tel: 0833 690606

Bradford Industrial Museum
Moorside Road
Eccleshill
Bradford BD2 3HP
Tel: 0274 631756

Dunrobin Castle
Golspie
Sutherland
Scotland
Tel: 04083 3177

Gladstone Pottery Museum
Uttoxeter Road
Longton
Stoke-on-Trent
Tel: 0782 311378

Jackfield Tile Museum
Jackfield
Telford
Shropshire
Tel: 0952 882030

Leighton House Art Gallery
12 Holland Park Road
London W14
Tel: 01-602 3316

Minton Museum
Minton Works
London Road
Stoke-on-Trent ST4 7QD
Tel: 0782 744766

Osborne House
York Avenue
East Cowes
Isle of Wight
Tel: 0983 200022

Victoria and Albert Museum
Cromwell Road
London SW7
Tel: 01-938 8500

RESTORATION

The Conservation Unit, part of the Museums and Galleries Commission, offers the Conservation Register, a database containing names and details of workshops and studios which provide specialized conservation and restoration services. For a small charge the Conservation Unit will send details of studios that can undertake ceramic tile restoration.

The Conservation Unit
Museums & Galleries Commission
7 St James's Square
London SW1Y 4JU

COLLECTING TILES

Royal Doulton International
Collectors' Club
167 Piccadilly
London W1
Tel: 01-491 2717

Phillips Fine Art Auctioneers
Blenstock House
7 Blenheim Street
New Bond Street
London W1Y 0AS
Tel: 01-629 6602

ADVISORY BODIES

British Ceramic Tile Council
Federation House
Station Road
Stoke-on-Trent ST4 2RU
Tel: 0782 747147

National Federation of Terrazzo/Mosaic
Specialists
Dickens House
15 Tooks Court
Cursitor Street
London EC4A 1LA
Tel: 01-831 7581

National Master Tile Fixers Association
Fairfax House
Fulwood Place
London WC1V 6DW
Tel: 01-405 8422

National Tile, Faience and Mosaic Fixers
Society
186 Goswell Road
Finsbury
London EC1V 7DT
Tel: 01-251 2251

Acanthus An herbaceous plant with prickly leaves, which, in a long, indented form, were copied to create a design of flowing, oval shapes with irregular edges, used on the capitals of columns. The acanthus leaf is a standard Greek motif, also used on tiles and mosaics.

Anthemion A Greek design based loosely on honeysuckle, with forms or lines radiating upwards and outwards from a base point. There is much variety within this basic design found on tiles, fabric, mouldings and throughout Greek decoration.

Arabesque A characteristically Islamic design, based on a geometrical grid, but using a curved, decorative line to create a flowing and intricate surface pattern.

Bolster chisel A cold chisel with a wide, flat blade, used with a club hammer to remove old tiles.

Carbide wheel Used for cutting through glass or ceramic.

Carborundum stone Used for sharpening knives and tools.

Chevron Repetitive 'V'-shape design.

Delftware Glazed earthenware, usually decorated with a distinctive blue on a white background, and originally made at Delft in Holland.

Diaper Ornamental architectural surface cover, often set in a diamond pattern.

Echinus A Greek design with egg-shaped or oval forms, alternating with thin vertical lines; often used in architectural moulding and around the upper part of a capital.

Greek Key (or fret) The most famous Greek design, consisting of vertical lines, with horizontals set at right angles, forming a repetitive, angular border ornamentation.

Grout Thin fluid mortar for filling interstices between tiles

Guilloche A simple decoration where curving lines form an entwined, circular, rhythmic design. The circles created by the design can be vacant, or can be further embellished.

Rococo Asymmetrical designs, using entwined and broken curves with crooked lines to create an extravagant, unorthodox design effect.

Rod saw A rod of carborundum that fits into a hacksaw and is used for cutting holes in ceramic.

Screed A piece of wood or plaster used for levelling floors.

Spacer pegs Pegs that you can buy or make from cardboard and which are fitted between tiles when they are laid, to ensure equal spacing between tiles. Many tiles come with spacer lugs which are like spacer pegs, but you may need to provide your own spacer pegs when laying floor tiles.

INDEX

BIBLIOGRAPHY

Elizabeth Eames, *English Medieval Tiles* (London, British Museum Publications, 1985).

F. Edward Hulme, *The Birth and Development of English Ornament* (New York, Macmillan 1894).

René Huyghe, general editor *Larousse Encyclopedia of Prehistoric and Ancient Art* (Paris 1957; London, Paul Hamlyn, 1962). Includes Claude Schaeffer's essay.

Owen Jones, *The Grammar of Ornament* (London 1856, reprinted 1986).

Spiro Kostof, *A History of Architecture* (O.U.P. 1985).

Nikolaus Pevsner, *Pioneers of Modern Design* (London, Peregrine 1987).

Robert Schmutzler, *Art Nouveau* (London, Thames & Hudson 1978).

Timothy Wilson, *Ceramic Art of the Italian Renaissance* (London, British Museum Publications 1987).

Acknowledgements
The photographs on the following pages were taken by Kirsty McClaren:
11, 14 bottom, 18, 20 bottom, 22 bottom left, 23, 30, 32 left, 33, 40, 44, 47, 54, 55, 58 top, 60, 61, 62, 63 right, 64, 65, 76, 78, 89 right, 91 top, 100, 101 bottom left, 103 bottom right, 106, 109, 118, 119, 120, 121, 124 right, 125.